C000173311

This book is a must-read if you...

- need some guidance to find your own path

- want inspiration from people from different walks of life from all over the world

- want to know how to beat the odds

- wish to immerse yourself in personal journeys of discovery

- want to uncover the secrets of positive thinking, passion and determination

- want to learn how to move forward with your life

"Fascinating stories of adaptation and resilience. A window into our complex, rich world. Down-to-earth voices, telling tales of self-discovery, self-challenge and self-compassion. Rewarding reading."

Ian Gregory Strachan

Associate Professor of English at The College of The Bahamas; Playwright; Poet; Novelist

"This book is a must-read. It is filled with stories of individual journeys and how to overcome adversity through self-determination and resilience.

We owe gratitude to those who are able to put their experiences in writing. It does not only inspire and empower others, but it helps to alleviate anxiety of how to cope and pursue their goals when faced with adversity. The lesson we learn comes from other people's experience.

When I reflect on my own journey, I can visualise how successful Adesola has used the compilation of individual stories to encourage the reflection of one's life and experience."

Dr Kate Anolue

Former Mayor of the London Borough of Enfield; Councillor; Author of 'Time for Purpose'

"This book is filled with wonderfully insightful lessons about life that make you richer in knowledge, wiser in experiences, stronger in will and determination, and mindful that this journey is all about unconditional love and acceptance of self, and when you focus on those mindful lessons, you see the true beauty and magic in all of life's experiences."

Diane Forster

TV Host & Podcaster – I HAVE TODAY with Diane Forster; 2020 Global Excellence Award Winner "Life Coach of The Year"; Bestselling Author 'I HAVE TODAY... Find Your Passion, Purpose & Smile... Finally!'

◊◊◊

"Being an anthologist myself, I completely echo this book and the experiences shared by the co-authors. Every chapter resonated with me.

For decades I have been trying to break barriers successfully, but by reading this book I have gained extra guidance and inspiration in finding my own path."

Dr Andrea Malam BEM

Award-winning Champion & Leader in Diversity; Charity Founder/Trustee; Author; Speaker; Anthologist

An eclectic collection
from contributors worldwide

LESSONS
LIFE HAS
TAUGHT ME

Stories that inspire change
and forge new paths

Compiled by
Adesola Orimalade

First published in Great Britain in 2023
by Book Brilliance Publishing
265A Fir Tree Road, Epsom, Surrey, KT17 3LF
+44 (0)20 8641 5090
www.bookbrilliancepublishing.com
admin@bookbrilliancepublishing.com

© Copyright Adesola Orimalade 2023

The moral right of Adesola Orimalade to be identified as the
author of this work has been asserted in accordance with the
Copyright, Designs and Patents Acts 1988.

All rights reserved. No part of this publication may be
reproduced, stored in a retrieval system, or transmitted, in any
form or by any means without the prior written permission of
the publisher, nor be otherwise circulated in any form of binding
or cover than that in which it is published and without similar
condition being imposed on the subsequent purchaser.

A CIP catalogue record for this book is available
at the British Library.

ISBN 978-1-913770-56-3

Typeset in Adobe Jenson Pro.
Printed by 4edge Ltd.

Lessons Life Has Taught Me

Foreword

"My mission in life is not merely to survive, but to thrive;
and to do so with some passion, some compassion,
some humour, and some style."
Maya Angelou

I love this quote by Dr Angelou. It is both a reminder and a call to action to not merely survive life, but to live life. In this pursuit, we are reminded to be mindful of what we represent, how we represent it and understanding our distinct identity, being and belonging that makes us unique. Taking the time to reflect and seeking clarity makes all the difference in merely being able to survive a moment or thriving for a lifetime.

My name is David Grevemberg and I have had the privilege and pleasure of living, for the most part, a life filled with curiosity, exploration, learning and plenty of opportunities for self-reflection, whether I realised it at the time or not. I have worked for over twenty-five years in the global sport and major events industry delivering proud moments and memories for people and their communities.

Having had the chance to extensively travel the world and explore so many fascinating cultures, I have built many meaningful friendships based on respect, mutual understanding, and learning. All these relationships have led me to discover, time after time, that there is much more that unites us than divides us, if we take the time to listen.

While my life has had its ups and downs – and yes, there have been plenty of moments I have been pulled side-to-side or even split right down the middle – I have always strived to be mindful of the ebbs and flows as part of a bigger journey of self-discovery and growth.

Whether it is the good, the bad, the great or the ugly, each teach us about what we value, the impact of the culture we create around us, and how our success or failure manifests themselves in our character (the decisions we make) and in our personality (how we project and communicate).

Through the inspirational leadership of Nina Bressler and Adesola Orimalade, I was privileged to be invited to reflect on this important compilation of reflections and contemplations captured in this book, *Lessons Life Has Taught Me.*

The assembly of this extremely diverse group of thought leaders represents an extensive and rich range of personal and professional lived experiences. Each author courageously articulates a lesson reflecting their human vulnerability and inspiration on a path to personal fulfilment and self-discovery. The span of experiences and expertise mastered by each of these contributors offers a rich mix of raw testimony that is timelessly relevant. Each author displays a distinctive style and approach to sharing their valuable insight.

In their own ways, with their own styles, they provide us with outlines of different shaped mirrors. The shape of each mirror is determined by each author's personal wisdom and unique life lessons. They beckon us to ask a very similar question when we look at our reflection in their mirror – where do I find purpose? And why?

Whether you are looking for inspiration on how to perform better, how to look at things from a different perspective or simply just reflecting on your identity, being and since of belonging – this book has something for you.

Thank you all so much – Adaeze Oreh, Adesola Orimalade, Amelia Samai-Nicome, Aysha Iqbal, Christopher Weguelin, Fatima Alimohamed, Gabrielle Botelho, Geri Maroney, Idowu Adebayo Thompson, Junjuan He, Kevin Tong, Lara Rogers, Minal Srivastava, Natalie Heilling, Natasha Preville, Nina Bressler, Shervonne Johnson and Susana Ecclestone – for your courage, openness, inspiration, and leadership in sharing some mindful lessons on what life has taught each of you.

David Grevemberg CBE

International Sports Executive
and Global Humanitarian

"These experiences … provide us with a source of light and hope in these trying times."

Adesola Orimalade

Introduction

In the year 2020, as we struggled to deal with the rules and the changes in lifestyle brought about by the pandemic, it suddenly occurred to me that even though as a society we were going through a collective trauma, we were also going through individual, very personal experiences.

At some point, the road to recovery looked infinite, and we couldn't see the light at the end of the tunnel. But we soon began to find strength in our own stories, and lessons life taught us.

These experiences, as unique and personal as they were, could provide us with a source of light and hope in these trying times. And it was this thought that kick-started the concept of *Lessons Life Has Taught Me*.

This led me down a path of deep reflection. Although the pandemic provided a major health challenge, in many ways, it also reflected the many other challenges we go through.

A Nigerian proverb says, "... the rain does not discriminate upon whom it falls ...". Imagine witnessing heavy rainfall. To a farmer, it may be the answer to prayers, yet to another farmer it would represent the destruction of harvests. Rainfall may affect a business as customers may not want to go shopping, yet there would be other businesses whose premises are damaged by the same rain.

We live the same event, but our experiences may be different.

However, I believed that we would come out at some point, and wanted to harness this experience into something positive.

So, I set out to capture stories that would inspire us and even start conversations on taking control of the present and looking forward to a brighter future. However, I didn't want to simply tell the story myself. I wanted others to tell their stories and, most notably, to select a lesson or lessons they gained from coming out on the other side.

That was what motivated me to write this book.

I also wanted the book to reflect the plurality of our world. Again, using the analogy of the rain, we live in different parts of the world, but we all cry, laugh, grieve, and mourn, and although these emotions may be dictated and influenced by our different cultures, there is a similarity in how these life events affect us.

Lessons Life Has Taught Me is a collection of stories and experiences compiled over the years to explore life's complexities – its highs and lows. Each contributor shares their golden thread stories, and as the anthologist,

I weave them into this compilation for you to enjoy. The stories come from different parts of the globe, some funny, some serious, and all relatable. It reflects my experiences and those of the esteemed co-authors who have chosen to be vulnerable in sharing their stories.

At this point, I pause to express my sincere appreciation to all my co-authors. They have walked and worked with me on this journey. You will meet seventeen of them, and I am genuinely humbled that they bought into the vision. You will get to read genuinely inspiring stories from the United Kingdom to Hong Kong, from the Bahamas to India, and from Nigeria to the United States.

In writing this book, I have discovered parts of myself, and given that I approached over 100 people to be a part of this project, I am pleased by the quality and depth of the stories we have shared here.

I have been motivated by the need to bring a smile to someone's face, provide an understanding of diversity and share experiences. It will all be worth it if I can help just one person on their journey.

When you have read each story in this book, you may think:

"I can relate to that!"

"I have experienced this too."

"Wow, that is a new perspective to consider."

Or just simply,

"What an inspiring story!"

You will no doubt find something here that speaks directly to **you** and your heart.

Welcome, and enjoy the journey!

Adesola Orimalade
December 2022

For the Doors that Never Opened …
I am Coming to Buy
the Whole Building!

Fatima Alimohamed

This will be a story that free-flows from one extreme end to the other, taking you through unique moments separated yet connected throughout, with common if not similar lessons.

A third-generation, born to a humble family of two different races and cultures on the sunny green continent of Africa, should be a good start for anyone, shouldn't it? As a child that was exposed to a home filled with very different cultures, races, and religions. The home where a one-eyed mother worked extremely hard with the government and knew all the dreaded fears plus perks that came with the role for her and the family, while the father was a businessman doing all that a father needed to do to prove society wrong on his choice of wife and to ensure that his family got the best of everything, especially in two specific areas: travelling the motherland and the world, as well as investing in education.

It is only much later in life that I learnt how these two areas would be crucial in this journey called life, both personally and professionally. Travelling opens one to a new way of seeing things and people. It makes one understand humanity, life, and more so that we are the same as much as we are different. Therefore, I question that if we are each unique and different, doesn't that mean we are all the same? On the other hand, education is crucial to eradicating poverty, poverty of the mind, spirit, knowledge, and, eventually, of pocket. One may have access to education, but that does not give one access to knowledge, whereas travelling and education together change one's perspective on life.

My journey started in a semi-private school environment where there was a balance in having fun whilst studying. The curriculum did not put as much pressure on young ones then, and there was a focus on both technical training and skills that would be of use at some point. While it was fun, skills were being embedded on how to cut cloth to stitch pyjamas, how to plant a vegetable patch and how to saw wood to make a stool. The technical skills were imparted to both boys and girls alike, with no superiority over the other. The journey from a private junior school to university in a foreign land was the first experience of how harsh the world out there was when your parents' umbrella doesn't cover you. Being a child of an African government employee, the choices were clearly defined and limited as to if you were to earn a scholarship, the options are chosen for you.

I landed in a country called India! The land of culture, spices, home to many religions, and the best education. It is no wonder Indians manage to be scouted for by top-notch firms as they house some of the best brains. Sadly, despite one part of me carrying half the ancestral blood, I experienced racism at first hand. A land that also showed me the audacity of the people who were my brothers from back home in Africa, selling me and my passport off to some turbaned bearded men for extra income. That is a longer story for another day!

I stayed back as I felt perhaps it was ignorance of individuals, not a nation, that was at the root of the racism, and perhaps desperation for students' survival was the root to sell one of their own? As I stayed back, destiny threw another curveball as the country underwent political challenges that led to the enforcement of government curfews.

The irony was that India was facing protests regarding setting up seats and quote reservations to redress the caste discrimination people faced in schools and jobs. So, as a foreigner, I was only getting to experience a deep-rooted problem they had faced internally for years. It wasn't easy being away from home trying to make your parents' dreams come true whilst trying to manoeuvre oneself with the harsh realities of life.

In this journey, I came out learning so much, making great friendships and, in the process, got immersed in some fantastic colourful cultures that have remained with me to date, that instilled a love for India that I keep wanting to discover more. Clearly, there is positivity in every adversity. My journey has been anything but dull, that's for sure.

My next phase of the journey took me to the late Queen of England's land, where I learned what being aloof, uninvolved, and cold meant. This was quite a contrast for someone coming from Africa, who lived in a part of Asia, where the warmth of people, foods, culture, and, of course, the weather was always about living life on the sunny side up.

The United Kingdom taught me what it meant to be on your own, surviving the rat race, to think of yourself first before anyone else and that it's a dog-eat-dog world out there. I never understood why it was not okay to look at someone whilst riding on the tube and smile. Why was it seen as invading someone's personal space if you put your hand out to help someone get on the bus? Life is interesting indeed. We get raised to learn to embrace and carry the Ubuntu Spirit along with us wherever we go. The same life then comes and teaches you that your cross is your own to carry and not the world's.

To be honest, I love what I learnt in the UK. It brought a sense of balance in my life where I learnt boundaries, detachment to emotions, and getting paid for how hard you are to replace and not how hard you work. I learnt the value of systems and process and that not everything works through connections and bribes, as it mostly does in Africa or India!

Before I could settle back home and decide what I was going to do with my life, an opportunity was staring me in the face to live and work in the Gulf region; Bahrain, to be specific. I applied for the job, not knowing if I would get it, and lo and behold, it was mine for the taking after a rigorous interview. Bags packed with no specific dreams in my eyes, I took off for the land of heavy perfume scents, streets with gold and Lamborghinis passing by!

Being raised a Muslim and now living in a predominantly Muslim country, you would have thought it would have been easy! What a culture shock I faced! Everything that I knew as a Muslim was slowly being shattered in front of my eyes.

In Africa, the 'dish dash' or white robe was signified with purity, prayers and respect, but in my new home, it was a daily attire even worn to nightclubs, and men partied easily in it! I was taken to private parties in sports cars I would never have dreamt of sitting in, had barbecues on private beaches, sailed on private yachts with people who had private lives. Wow! But when prayer time called, shops closed, people prayed, and afternoon siesta was a norm after that, and when all is up, the night will continue like it was a day. Seeing gold shops lined up with kilos of gold vests, bangles, even gold robes, made me sick to the point where I cannot appreciate gold, and I am still put off it even today.

This journey taught me that money does indeed make the world go round, but you can't eat money at the end of the day. So, after a year or so, feeling like everything around me was inauthentic – from the imported grass to the forced glam looks and brands being shown off – I packed my bags to go back to my family as my heart felt I was living in an unreal world. I was reported as AWOL since I just upped and left. I guess in life, there comes a time when your heart and soul decide what sits well with your conscience, and once that decision is made, there is no turning back.

I smile as I write all this down. The memories of my journey have been worth a lot. The lessons, the friendships, and the choices all kept me on my toes. I was and continue to be a discoverer of life. I can now safely reference myself to a royalty dish called the biryani! I love food, and the biryani would be the perfect analogy. If you have never tried it, then you haven't lived. A biryani takes hours to prepare, lots of tolerance, patience, vast ingredients, and a specialised art to make it. Some ingredients must be brought together, and others cooked or flavoured separately before being layered to make this one-pot dish. I am like the biryani: some whole spices that, if you bite into, you will be repelled; some caramelised onions that are fried to bring out sweetness rather than the pungent flavour they are known for; rice that in some spots will be as white as snow; and in other flavours, tainted with colours of bright red or sunburst orange, and mint to bring sweetness as the tongue experiences the spiciness of the chillies. A dish packed with a history and a prior journey, served in front of kings and queens!

Coming back home to the motherland was the next phase of life. The stage where one is confused and asks, "What next?" I had been used to so much freedom, the experience of making my own decisions, living with no future or commitments in my head. Was I now ready to get serious and settle down with a career and perhaps a family? Despite it being home, everything apart from my family felt alien. I felt trapped to join the mundane rat race of life that everyone robotically seemed to join naturally; find a job, get married, and the rest will flow.

This free spirit did just that! I found a job that became the line that I then stuck with today: marketing. Well, in those days, it was in one facet of marketing which was the advertising part that I lived. I loved it and made lifetime friends who today are my inner and most trusted circle. It was a glam job where there was cut-throat competition for creativity and awards honouring the best crafts. Being able to walk into a boardroom mainly in those days dominated by men and getting their undivided attention was like winning a trophy. You must have heard of that song by Yazz in the eighties titled *The Only Way Is Up*. That title was meant for me. Every year I was promoted and every year I learnt something new and invested in myself.

Then came the period where I looked around and realised that everyone had 'moved on' and started settling down except for me. What was I going to do? I was too busy growing in my career to pay attention to those who were desperately wooing me. I was no doubt a stunning woman. This was when I made the biggest and perhaps the only mistake in my life; getting married to my friend, not because I was in love but because I thought I was in love and perhaps of the fear that there was going to be no one else left around to marry.

Mistakes never last too long. One has to learn from them, dust oneself off, and that is what I did. I filed for divorce and focused my life on caring for my parents and to raise my daughter single-handedly. If one were to ask me if I had any regrets, my answer would be "none whatsoever". I learned my lessons hard, but I got a beautiful and amazing daughter from my marriage and a lifelong purpose. There was no stopping me from forging forward.

I continued to soar and take on challenges head-on professionally as well as caring for my parents, especially my father, who became my priority because of his ailing health. As my siblings continued to study in the UK, I took the responsibility to shoulder the home and balance my personal life at home, my professional life at work, and my social life with my daughter and friends. At some point, it was going to take its toll, and it did. I suffered a brain infarct and was paralysed, but that didn't stop me from receiving work in my hospital bed. I am a firm believer that when you believe you are ill in your mind, that is when everything crumbles. I fought every negative thought and only focused on getting better.

Within three weeks, I was back at work, and I remember in four days of leaving the hospital, I was on stage with my colleagues from work to receive several awards on behalf of the company.

Like with every phase in an organisation, it was time to move on and spread my wings. My wings took me away once again from family to the shores of Lake Victoria in Uganda, where my fast-paced life calmed down, and I got used to the village life in Jinja and made amazing friends who are family to date. I have to admit I only agreed to go to Uganda thanks to a friend, whom I refer to as SG, who convinced me and my family to take this leap of faith. It became another home where even the supermarket owner knew me so well that I could pick my groceries anytime and pay when I wanted! My daughter got first-hand experience of homeschooling and perhaps had the best life ever where it was all-natural and just us.

On achieving what was to be done, I was asked to shuttle between Ivory Coast and Uganda, then finally asked to settle in Ghana to set up the team's operations. On achieving significant success and with many lessons, I left the organisation, primarily because I learnt that your value when employed is only worth the towing of the line that you do. Loyalty, integrity, and sacrifice will never be considered at the forefront.

There was something in the air about Ghana that I was pulled back to, to start African Brand Warrior, a consultancy firm with a close and dear family friend, whom I will refer to as RT, who supported me unconditionally in the journey of entrepreneurship.

Coming back to Ghana was also a way for the Universe to say "You need to be honoured for the queen that you truly are". I was stooled as a Queen Mother of the Memia Palace in Western Ghana and years later I was again stooled as a Queen Mother for HoeHoe in the Volta region. This may be hard to believe, but I recalled an interview in a magazine in 2005 where I had said I was a queen, and who knew that one day I would manifest the title, the crown and stool in reality!

Hopefully, in some other chapter or a future book, I will share the pains that humans caused me in the later journey of my life too. Life lessons that have been learnt the most painful way teaching me that there are those you may have genuinely loved and considered as family but they came to remind me that if they are not blood, they will truly never consider one as family.

How those you considered friends too could flip in a second, and turn against you for their own selfish reasons.

Surprisingly, in the very same breath, other humans taught me that family doesn't have to be blood and I continue to be grateful for them.

Each phase and each journey shaped who I was becoming and sharpened my thoughts while moulding me to become a human that would quickly adapt to any environment and situation. I started understanding what 'being' human was rather than just being called a human being. I was meant to be. To be alive, to be alert, to be happy, to be content.

I know for a fact, if a door doesn't open for me, God always has a way of making me come back to buy the entire building armed with lessons learned!

Lifelong Learning

Kevin Tong

I was not a straight-A student at school. In fact, I had difficulty concentrating and was not performing well. I would probably have what is called ADHD today. Despite this, I became an entrepreneur and built a successful wealth management business from scratch. How did that hyperactive child gain focus and become a successful entrepreneur?

I believe the central principles are continuous learning and perseverance through challenges. I would like to share the experiences and lessons I have learned from education and lifelong learning in the hope these lessons may benefit others.

The lessons start from my childhood. I switched from a Chinese school system to studying in Cameroon and

Switzerland, enabling me to learn to speak fluent French and English, and ultimately gain Swiss citizenship and job opportunities. The lessons are also from my university studies.

Despite my challenges with learning French as a Chinese speaker, I attended one of the world's best hotel management schools and gained valuable experience working in restaurant kitchens. The lessons continued into my professional studies, obtaining one of the most prestigious financial qualifications, CFA, and an MBA from one of the world's top business schools, which was essential in developing my career from a private banker to building my own business. Throughout, my dedication to sports (for example, I possess ski and snowboard instructor qualifications) was instrumental in helping me gain focus in my education.

Childhood

As a child being born and growing up in Taiwan, I was very hyperactive. I had difficulty concentrating, which meant I was not performing well in school. As one extreme example, I was so disruptive to other students that the teacher asked my mother to sit with me in the classroom for a week.

This problem was compounded at age ten when my family moved to Cameroon for business. I enrolled in a French school and switched from a Chinese system to a

French system. All of my lessons were in French. I only spoke Chinese and did not even know the alphabet. Despite extra private tutoring in French, which I endured even during the school holidays, it was difficult to catch up. Ultimately, since my parents were busy with work and did not speak French, at age thirteen, they sent me to boarding school in Switzerland to give me a better future.

In the early nineties, few Chinese people were travelling overseas. At age thirteen, I became the first and only Chinese student in my boarding school. Besides my difficulties with studying, I had to adapt to a new life, being with other children constantly and sometimes facing cultural discrimination problems. Looking back, I was very fortunate to attend this school because I discovered my passion for sports. I experienced many sports including mountain climbing, cross-country running, tennis, basketball, and skiing. I did not think I had a particular talent in any of the sports.

However, I was very competitive and dedicated and would stay later than other children to train for competitions. I had the most success in skiing. I started as a complete beginner at age thirteen and had never seen snow before. I remember having a terrible crash against a tree during ski training and my nose bleeding. However, I persevered during my training and practised harder than other students. I ended up surpassing some other children who had been skiing since age five and even won competitions as part of the ski competition team.

Through sports, my life at boarding school improved. I found common interests with other students and made friends, despite the cultural differences. My studies improved as I spent my extra energy on sports, which meant I concentrated better in class. I realised I could achieve challenging goals by planning a logical strategy and consistently working hard to improve and reach these goals. This lesson would stay with me throughout my life.

Although my French had progressed significantly by the time of my final secondary school exams, my French was still not as good as those of my classmates who were native speakers, and therefore I failed the exams. This failure was devastating, as I had to repeat my final year when all my peers graduated. I would count this as my first colossal failure in life. After the summer passed, I decided not to let this defeat me. I studied harder than ever. On my second try, I passed the exams and achieved the grades needed to attend my dream university, École Hôtelière de Lausanne (EHL), one of the leading hotel management schools in the world.

University Learning

After the initial joy of being accepted to EHL, reality set in. The training programme at EHL was extremely intense. Not only in terms of studies, but also physically. On a typical day, I would study in the classroom for around six hours, then work in a kitchen for six hours.

To fit in my homework, I would study very early in the morning or late at night, then wake up early the next day for kitchen or service work. The same values I had learnt through my sport and language studies were reinforced at EHL. I would need to work hard every day to progress from the bottom to the top gradually.

My biggest challenge during my time in university was not only work and studies, but it was also in my second year when my father suddenly passed away from a brain injury. It was a pain that makes you want to give up everything and just close up to the world. I was away from school for a few weeks because of this tragedy, and I wanted to stop school for a while. I finally tried to overcome this pain and keep pursuing my studies, as I knew this was what my father would want me to do.

Professional Life

My learning has continued throughout my professional life. Applying the same principles I had learnt through sport, I knew that to progress in my career I would need to keep progressing in learning.

As a graduate, I found my first job as a teaching assistant at EHL. I felt tremendous pressure, going from a struggling student to standing before a class as a teacher. I would teach both the French and English sections. I had only learnt English as a third language at boarding school. To overcome these challenges, I devoted time before each class to prepare, which meant I could answer the students' questions. It became clear that to succeed in my career, preparation and continuous learning are essential.

This lesson would be valuable when my next opportunity arose. One of the most prestigious private banks in Geneva selected me for a training programme to become a private banker. I was fortunate that this bank was seeking a candidate to grow its Asia business. I was in a perfect position given my language skills (Chinese, French and English), which were unusual in Switzerland, and having already obtained Swiss citizenship.

To improve my investment knowledge in this role, I pursued a CFA qualification. CFA is renowned as one of the most prestigious and demanding financial qualifications. The qualification comprises three levels, and the pressure to pass was intense. The level 1 exam could only be taken twice a year, and level 2 and 3 could only be taken once a year.

The biggest challenge was that exam preparation was done in parallel with my full-time job. I spent countless hours studying in the evening after work and on weekends. While studying, I was also adjusting to the challenges of relocating from Geneva to the bank's Hong Kong office, dealing with new professional responsibilities and pressures.

Despite my efforts, I failed twice. I felt defeated and thought several times about giving up. However, I remembered times when I had failed in studies or sport in the past but had overcome these failures. I persevered and finally obtained my CFA qualification.

All these lessons were essential at the later stage of my career when I became an entrepreneur and built my own business. Continuous learning would be essential for the success of my business. I enrolled in an EMBA programme while working full-time, developing my technical investment knowledge, developing soft skills, and building new business connections. I enrolled in the programme at the University of Chicago Booth School of Business, known for being rigorous and highly demanding.

Many of my classmates struggled with the programme's intensity and balancing their studies with work and family life. However, from my previous experiences, I was well equipped to deal with the challenges and handle my studies.

Conclusions

I believe there is an essential factor of chance and destiny beyond my control across each stage of my learning journey. However, I would like to share some overall lessons that can contribute to success in life.

Lesson 1: Have challenging goals, and do not be afraid of the difficult path

Although the French language school system was more challenging than the English system, it allowed me to ultimately obtain Swiss citizenship and an exceptional job opportunity in Switzerland. By comparison, my sister attended the English language system and even performed better at school. It was, however, difficult for her to find a job in the US since there were too many other English-speaking Chinese students competing for jobs.

Furthermore, after graduating, it would have been easier not to pursue further education but I chose to pursue my CFA and EMBA which ultimately helped me to succeed in my career and business.

Lesson 2: Life is a marathon, not a sprint. Take one step at a time and continually move forward

Life is a long journey. You do not need to be the best at everything from the start. It is more important to be persistent and continually work hard towards your goals.

Although some of my friends excelled in school, over time, I progressed further in my accomplishments.

This success is because I always continued progressing and pursued further education. For instance, the CFA requires significant demands on your time, so some professionals choose not to take the exams. However, the CFA has been invaluable as the basis for my investment knowledge.

Lesson 3: Whenever you face downturns and failures in life, never give up

I have faced many failures and downturns, whether dealing with a tragedy or failing an exam. I have often considered giving up. However, I always remind myself of what my father used to say: "What is important in life is not the result, but the process you went through." Have you tried hard enough and given your best? If yes, you cannot have regret, even if you fail.

Looking back, the most significant impact on me and the most memorable experiences are not the results I achieved in sports, education, or work. It is the process that I endured through hard work, dedication and sometimes failures, which made these experiences more valuable.

Lesson 4: Pursue hobbies and interests

From childhood until today, my passion is sports. Sports have helped me build a strong, healthy body, which is fundamental. In times of stress and failures, I use sports to release my stress, clear my head, and resume work with better concentration and productivity. Through sports, I have learned essential principles for success, such as teamwork, perseverance, dedication and recovering from failures.

Studies and work may not bring you happiness but are unavoidable. It is important to pursue hobbies and interests to learn principles that apply to your career and life. This could be sports, music, or art, but it should be something you are passionate about and want to excel in.

Changing Perspectives

Aysha Iqbal

The decision I made to relocate to the West Country region in the UK as a reporter and news anchor for an extensive television network was a transformative experience on so many levels. As a young professional woman in my twenties, I made this decision; looking back now, it was quite interesting, even before you have the added complication of being from an ethnic minority background. I know pretty well that what I have described above would not amount to an "earth-shaking life event" in the grand scale of things and compared to some experiences others have had. However, I would say that it wasn't a usual standard career move that many would have contemplated, let alone made.

Leaving my urban landscape in London to live in Devon and pursue my dream career gave me life experiences that would ultimately remould, shape, and change many of the materialistic value systems I had believed in and lived as a young Londoner. Now, before you put different shades of colour on the term "materialistic," let me put that term into context.

London is an expensive city to live in, and even if you only worked in the city and are one of the millions who commute in for work, London is still an expensive city. Part of that viewpoint is simply because the cost of living is relatively high. You are expected to dress with style, and even basic items like lunch at the gastropub or bistro round the corner can be expensive in many corporate roles.

Many of my friends were also preoccupied with a lifestyle comprising fashion, trends, and living the high life. The latest designer handbag, holidays to trendy locations, and driving the latest cars were subjects dear to their hearts. This is a mindset I was slowly slipping into and would have slipped into if I had stayed in the city at this impressionable young age.

Soon after I settled in Devon, I bought a flat in the port city of Plymouth, just five minutes from the harbour and beach and close to the fabulous Devon countryside. My extended family and friends back home in the big city were meanwhile contemplating their moves into more plush locations like Highgate and Chelsea. Rather than spending all my spare time shopping as I usually did in London, on my days off work in Devon, I would visit the local beach and harbour as well as the eye-opening, jaw-dropping, and stunning countryside locations.

It offered me time to appreciate nature and to reflect and contemplate on lighter issues. Rather than dreaming of the latest designer handbag, I found myself enjoying the simplicity and beauty of the stunning nature that surrounded me. Whilst I was using my "me time" to get familiar with the sights and sounds of Devon and Cornwall, my reporting work also gave me many amazing experiences.

The assignments I covered, albeit not as glamorous as the ones I had worked hard for in London, had lots of local angles to them. From travelling to cover post office closure protests in picture-postcard villages, to sailing in a speedboat into the ocean to film a boat race, to having a day spent at sea with the RNLI (Royal National Lifeboat Institution), these assignments allowed me to see life in a different perspective. And breaking free from my "materialistic mindset," my work as a news anchor and journalist was pushing my confidence levels to new limits. The multiple changes in my life meant I was developing and becoming a better, more content, and authentic individual. In short, leaving behind the safety and the "rat race" of London, I was becoming a better version of myself.

Now and in many periods over the last few years, I have contemplated my life journey. I am pretty confident that had I stayed in London building a career in the news media, I would have most likely become more engrossed in being "looks conscious," "status conscious," and imbibed a culture that has trapped many in the rat race.

My surroundings and new friendships were, however, forcing me to grow. After most weekends, I had colleagues who would tell me of their sailing expeditions, others who were hiking on their days off work, whilst some colleagues would look forward to having a family picnic at one of the West Country's stunning beaches. My cameraman colleague, Gareth, would delightfully inform me (on our van drives to filming locations) how he had spent his Sundays working for a local charity.

These differed significantly from the conversations I would have in London, which would more than likely focus on consumerism and superficial fluff. I learnt from my colleagues that you should live to work to live, and not live to work.

On my many journeys to filming locations with cameramen, they would tell me of their disdain for London, sounding almost repulsed as they referred to London's traffic, pollution, and enormous crowds. One of the cameramen, Simon, who once had a successful editing business in London, would often tell me how much more content living in Devon he was and how he enjoyed Devon's natural beauty and more peaceful pace of life. I was also inspired by how my colleagues spent weekends having picnics, sailing, and doing charity work. Their authenticity was also very infectious. Gradually, by being in their company, I began dropping my defences.

When not presenting on-air, I started wearing less make-up, felt the need to shop less frequently and started exploring hobbies and pastimes in nature. I also became more involved in charity work.

After living in the West Country for nine years, I got married to a guy from London, and it was time to move back and embark on marital life. Rather than slipping back to my old ways, I now felt detached from a highly materialistic way of life. It was great being back near family and my old friends, but I was no longer the same person. Rather than getting my nails done or obsessing over the latest outfit, I found these things held less importance to me.

I visited the Surrey countryside on weekends with my husband. Although I had been born in Surrey, I had never ventured into the countryside, having in the past been more dazzled by the lights of central London. Now I felt great solace and peace being surrounded by nature and discovered unique countryside gems near to my home.

Rather than valuing the latest designer labels, I also found myself investing in my relationships rather than things. It became more important to me to connect with my friends on a deeper and more authentic level than just needing to impress them.

I also began to value the time I spent with my parents, perhaps influenced by my family-oriented peers in Devon. Whenever driving through a scenic village or passing by the countryside, I am always family-oriented, whisked back to memories of my time in Devon and Cornwall, a picturesque time in my life, where I learned and grew so much.

After a sixteen-year career in the media and having presented thousands of live bulletins and reported on hundreds of stories, returning to London, I desired to start my own company. Television was an exciting industry, but one that is very consuming and highly competitive. I soon realised that I wanted more time to spend on the things I loved and to spend more time with the people I loved.

Having taken a quick break from broadcasting, I began my own company, Wizz Media, a media filming and training business. I never expected it to take off so soon and so suddenly, but I realised that this offered me the best work-life balance and enabled me to teach and coach, which are personal passions of mine.

Today I choose to work part-time yet still earn much more than I did in journalism, but most importantly, it allows me to be myself, work in my own time and be my own boss. I have not ruled out returning to a sixteen-year broadcasting career. Still, as each day passes and as my business grows, the opportunities opening up for me are those I would never have expected, and this is a new adventure and chapter in my life.

When I see young people today in the rat race, I feel grateful I was given the opportunity to be challenged in my views and opinions, and the reality check the West Country gave me. For many of my friends in London, their lives are still primarily motivated by materialism, but I have also met new friends who share some of my more authentic values.

Be Your Own Cheerleader

Lara Rogers

We are exposed to so many influences in our lifetime, and it's hard to find out why we have adopted certain approaches or working styles. Some may stem from our moral code, our early training, or the nature of our current work environment. I choose to share a life lesson grown from roots planted in my belief system even before my career began. These roots spread and managed to be a significant influence over my career for many years. They took hold during my education...

I was a bright student who excelled in several subjects. I enjoyed many aspects of school, not simply learning new things, but what I saw as the admirable way they recognised hard work and ability. It was clear cut. If you worked hard and achieved good grades, reward and recognition came your way. As one of the top students in my year, both at school and university, I became familiar with receiving praise for what was essentially my output. My teachers, lecturers, and even members from industry I met when representing the school, all appeared to note my ability, and I duly received opportunities.

I represented the school at a Ford CRAC Understanding Industry course, and the Ford representative asked that I contact them at the end of my A-Levels as they would be interested in employing me. The local newspaper editor said they would accept me as a journalist after writing several articles for them whilst still at school. I was a form representative and nominated by my teachers to sit Special Papers. By the time I was eighteen, I was convinced that the vital ingredients for success were hard work and 'technical' ability.

Fast forward several years, and I had carried these same expectations into the workplace. During this early stage of my career, I felt my hard work approach and achieving my work targets continued to pay off. By the age of twenty-one, I was a manager, and over the next decade, I received rapid promotions in every role I held. When my line managers changed roles or left the company in three consecutive positions, the senior leadership team proactively promoted me to take over their position.

In one of these roles, a peer gave me the most surprising feedback I had received to date – they told me I worked too hard! They pointed out that they often did the minimum work possible, which allowed them to have more fun with their team, but more importantly, it freed up time for them to focus on their relationship with the senior leadership.

I had already noticed that they certainly took their own advice, as often the person in question would sit there surfing the net, chatting to his girlfriend, and joking around. I was far from impressed! I also noticed that he always looked busy when the senior directors were around and invested significant time in talking to them. Sometimes about work, sometimes about life in general, not just forming and establishing a relationship but investing in self-promotion. I would hear him tell them how he had met or surpassed his target, how he had implemented a new process, how he was pleased because his client had provided some positive feedback.

In contrast, while I had achieved the highest gross profit, I had significantly grown my account revenue and had the top client retention rate. I knew the CEO received this information in their reports. It never occurred to me to mention this to them directly. I would have felt uncomfortable in doing so, as I saw it as bragging.

Conversely, I was very thoughtful about the time I invested in my team, arranging social events, implementing clear personal development plans, and ensuring I took the time to know them individually. Over the years, I have watched these team members progress in various sectors. I am pleased to count many of them as friends and proud that several of them two decades later still turn to me for business advice – even though several of them are now in very senior positions.

Shortly after this conversation with my colleague, I was headhunted and left to join another organisation. My ex-colleague remained at my previous company and was promoted more than once during their time at the organisation. They now hold a very senior position for a large BPO organisation.

As I progressed into more senior roles, they became more strategic. I was thoughtful about the engagement and support I had with my teams. I gave regard to cultivating excellent relationships with my clients but spent no real time considering how best I engage with my direct line manager or the C suite. Upwards management was where my strategic planning stopped!

I have helped many colleagues, direct reports, and managers succeed throughout the years, but I have remained silent about the support I have given them in most instances. This has ranged from ghostwriting articles for international magazines, troubleshooting to help leaders overcome issues, or simply working late alongside them to meet their deadlines. This natural approach to helping others is what I felt was right – give, not to receive...

This behaviour made me friends but did not help my career. One of my bosses, a lady herself, gave me a book called *Nice Girls Don't Get the Corner Office* by Lois P Frankel.

By this point in my career, I realised that I still found it difficult to promote myself and I struggled with peers who overly invested in this approach. For example, I would not see one colleague I worked with in the office for weeks when our Vice-President was overseas, only for them to return to the office the same day our VP returned from their travels. On such days, they'd work harder than they had in the six weeks they were gone! Somehow, I viewed this as cheating in a test and I had little respect for this colleague. While this behaviour may be extreme, the underlying message was there for me to see, but I simply was not ready to take it onboard! I needed to become strategic in my upward management and get comfortable with self-promotion.

I am not alone in being uncomfortable with self-promotion. Research conducted in 2013 by Barbara Annis and Associates, in partnership with Thomson Reuters and Women of Influence, demonstrated that women struggle in this area. As published by Forbes, they attributed notable challenges to career advancement to "... both navigating the system and accessing informal networks. The challenge is in self-promotion, advocating for themselves, and expressing their talents."

Women tend to not talk about their accomplishments, and when they do, the focus is often on historical achievements rather than highlighting their future potential.

A more recent study undertaken in 2019 by the Harvard Business Review also found a significant gender gap in self-promotion. Citing that men rate their performance 33% higher than equally performing women, the various study versions revealed that confidence or strategic incentives did not drive this gender gap. They revealed that even though men and women performed equally well on the test, men rated themselves an average of 61 out of 100, while women only rated themselves a 46 out of 100. They also discovered that self-promotion makes a difference, with workers who rated their performance more highly on the 0–100 scale being more likely to be hired and offered a greater salary.

Times are changing, and I believe social media has helped many young people think of their 'personal brand.' I would advise those who are just starting their careers or are at a challenging point in their career, to focus on understanding their own value proposition. This is essentially the unique way in which you deliver work that contributes to positive business outcomes. Once you understand this, it provides a solid foundation for authentic self-promotion.

Think strategically about how you will self-promote. Think in terms of how, what, and why. How will you raise awareness of your achievements in a way that will not make you appear a braggart? Who will you self-promote to? Why are you self-promoting? What outcomes do you want?

In terms of tips for successful self-promotion, Forbes recommends aligning your value proposition with others' goals and interests. The result is they know how you affect positive business results, and you are now on their radar screen for future opportunities. Positioning yourself as part of a solution is effective self-promotion because you base it on past achievements and future potential.

I believe it remains essential to differentiate between having the confidence to communicate your successes from the 'office politics' approach of self-promotion, whereby one does less but sells oneself more! Perceived success without actual achievement would be akin to building a tower block on shaky foundations – it may reach heady heights in the short term, but it will fall at some point. In contrast, if you are good at your job, having visibility at work can be critical to longer-term progression and cross-team trajectory.

I would advise the younger me that successfully navigating the workplace requires more than just ability and hard work. You must be politically savvy to self-promote effectively. You need to build your knowledge of workplace dynamics and be committed to building strategic relationships. This differs from friendships.

It is about developing the ability to craft conversations with those people who have power and influence so that they buy into you, your ideas, your brand!

Building relationships with the senior leadership team is an undeniably important way to progress. Many executives are more accessible to company employees than ever before, offering mentoring and open-door policies. These are great opportunities to gain visibility, and all importantly, learn from those with more experience than yourself. These interactions can help you improve your performance and proffer an opportunity for feedback on the results you attain through their guidance – an authentic way to communicate your achievements.

Empowering others also empowers you! One slight bugbear I have had over the years is seeing how managers and some leaders take direct credit for their team members' work. My advice here is simple – if you support others, help them perform, and give them what they need to do well; this is a great way to show you have done an excellent job! If you have hired talented people and provided them with an environment where they can deliver great things, that is an excellent testament to you being a skilled manager. Whilst I do not advocate being silent about your successes, sometimes results really do speak for themselves.

Sharing your knowledge and offering support toward colleagues can be another effective tool that shows the value you bring to the organisation. This may take the form of sharing your expertise or even offering emotional and motivational support that lifts others when they are jaded or overawed. I have lost count of the times I have had to sit down with a colleague or even senior directors, late at night, when they were tired and up against a deadline, simply helping them complete their task. Maybe you and your colleague will be the only ones who ever know you did this, but this is one way you create advocates who will support you and be vocal about your worth.

It is therefore worth remembering that, no matter what your position in the organisation, self-promotion is critical to your success. Take pride in sharing your achievements, think about what you bring to the organisation, and do not undersell yourself! Be strategic, have a plan, and you will succeed.

Do not leave how others view you to chance – be your own cheerleader.

Situation, Task, Action, Result

Idowu Adebayo Thompson

As logical beings, we often assume that our ambitions, individual traits, competencies, and corporate opportunities intertwine to define our career progression, defining how far and quickly we move, and in turn the sense of fulfilment that we derive from our work lives.

Real-life experience may, however, prove to be more deviant. There are those whom may seem to run the career race decisively, self-guided, but too quickly, burning out well before they can ever achieve their full potential. Others experience repeated frustrations as they rest on fate and doing what they feel are the "right things" to advance their career growth.

Such would often complain about the absence of fair opportunities or reciprocal rewards by their employers in return for the years of hard work and complete dedication to their jobs. Unfortunately, while some are privileged to have formal or informal mentor figures in the background, providing guidance through the unfamiliar terrain and the occasional emotional self-doubt moments, others have had to stumble through unguided, relying on their first-hand experiences to define how they react to situations.

Reminiscing over the last two decades of my work life, I realise that while I had made some excellent decisions, I had also had my fair share of mistakes, with each becoming a learning opportunity that has further shaped my growth. Work for me has probably become the most dominant part of my ephemeral life, as the hours accounted for by this activity had grown, and with time and seniority.

Outside this, the work culture I had become acquainted with in more recent years has the line between work and personal life becoming less indecipherable. Life has indeed taught me several invaluable lessons around work and relationships in particular.

Finding Your Passion

As I spent a significant part of my work life split between two countries with repeated exposure to several others through work assignments, I realised pretty early the importance of finding my strengths and concentrating my efforts on driving-related competencies. I would admit it wasn't that easy, nor did it happen that quickly. While I felt reasonably comfortable with figures in high school, I also had an equal pull for the more self-expressive subjects and yearned for direction that anchored both. In the eighties, after the initial struggles of convincing my late father, who was a medical doctor, that the route to medicine wasn't the path for me, with the invaluable help of my eldest sister and brother, who were both trained doctors, I found it easier thereafter planning my career, as I no longer had to contend with the subtle pressures of living up to what were expectations of the last child of six.

My career subsequently evolved into banking, covering roles from foreign currency trading to wealth management, making it easier for me to apply my technical competencies gained through formal and informal learning and relationship skills.

For me, I had completed the full circle. I had learned that finding one's strengths is one thing, while developing job-relevant competencies around such strengths is just as important. Over the years, I had also been acquainted with a few commonly-held beliefs related to our work lives.

Belief 1

Senior Management or Executive levels roles downplay technical competencies while emotional intelligence rules.

My thoughts are non-prescriptive but would suggest that you need a measure of both. There is, however, no natural substitute for competence (distinct from paper qualifications). Competence gaps are sometimes covered up by having the next layer with the requisite skill; however, this may not be a sustainable strategy. There is also nothing wrong with having a competence gap. What is wrong is doing absolutely nothing to redress and close the gap noted.

Belief 2

You need a Board or Executive level sponsor to succeed in senior C level roles.

This appears to be a widely accepted message reinforced by some leading motivational speakers. Naturally, the stronger the Executive/Board level support, the stronger the prospects for success.

The reality, though, is that outside of the intricacies and complexities often defined by the interests of the key stakeholders and promoters, the organisation's success remains a converging goal for all. Though these sponsors can help drive visibility, they also look out for individuals who can deliver on the job. Results rule.

From the Shop Floor

I started my banking career in the early nineties. I often struggled to keep the balance between being emotive and yet effective as a leader. There is a natural inclination to be liked and sometimes trading off effectiveness.

I remember several years back interviewing a young man for a middle-management role. At the interview, I noticed he was only wearing one sock. I drew his attention to this briefly, and with a smile on his face, he explained that he had rushed out of the house to beat the traffic and that he had virtually finished dressing up in the dark as there was a power outage in his building (some can relate to this).

I hired him, though. At that point, I must admit I had my initial concerns.

I remember our banter when I would correct memos he wrote. He would tell me how he felt my standards were super elevated and how he was a prize winner in school where he was acclaimed as a prolific writer. We developed a genuine friendship on and off the job and would even hang out for drinks from time to time (a conversation for another day).

Undoubtedly he showed solid relationship skills on the job quickly, though not one to be conscripted by stifling structure or routine of work. Much later, he moved on to another institution where the job role provided the flexibilities he had always wished for in a job.

We still find time to catch up from time to time, and while I have continued setting high work expectations, I soon realised that it is more important to develop people by setting the proper examples, holding myself accountable to the same standards. I have also learned the role of well-placed empathy distinct from permissiveness, that encourages ineffectiveness.

The same employees we work with are mothers, fathers, breadwinners, and much more at home. I have learned that as leaders, we should have a sincere concern for the well-being of our teams and not a notional speak.

I have also learned the value of open and direct conversations driven by the genuine desire to make things better. Leadership is like a football game with several coaches on the sideline. As I have found, a few will misunderstand and even dislike you, but those who appreciate your sincerity and work ethics are those that will remain your raving fans years after.

Self-Confident Arrogance?

Back to Nigeria from the UK, sometime in the early nineties, after my postgraduate studies, I had my first serious experience job hunting. The natural options as it appeared then were careers either in banking or the oil and gas industry.

At this time, the banking industry 'at home' appeared to be going through its initial growth phase. The sector was one of the top in terms of salaries and benefits, and the glamour and attraction of managing other people's money made it a natural choice for me in some ways. I was sending out copies of my résumé to companies, family, and personal contacts. I had a few interviews scheduled and remember vividly one which stuck.

I recall walking confidently, smartly dressed in a pinstripe blue wool suit, with the swirls of the Oud perfume I had on trailing me mildly. I had read about the bank and had tried to prepare myself as much as I could for this. I was directed into the meeting room where the session was scheduled, and I saw five men sitting around the meeting room table staring at me. I found this momentarily discomfiting, but soon put the feeling behind me.

The initial introductions were made, and they threw several questions at me, including some from my first-degree programme. I felt everything had gone reasonably well until the Human Resources department representative asked about my salary expectations.

Having done some research on the levels of relevant salaries, I responded. Suddenly, one of the panel members burst out laughing. I didn't think this was very professional but ignored it.

Another now asked more civilly if I didn't think this was too high, to which I had responded, "No" and then explained why I felt this wasn't the case. Before I could round up, I heard another panel member say in a local language, "This boy is not serious and doesn't seem to need a job." He probably assumed I didn't understand, but at that point, I had told myself that I would remain polite and controlled, so I thanked them for the interview and left the room.

In some ways, it was a culture shock for me, and I must assume I was thrown back by their actions but had decided that I would keep my self-confidence.

About three weeks later, I received a written job offer from the same bank. Still, I had already decided that if what I had experienced at the interview in any way reflected how employees are or would be treated, then I would instead find the organisation with the right culture fit for me. Several weeks later, I eventually got through a highly reputable institution's test and job interview and became a Management Trainee.

Years later, the first bank had ceased to exist, subsumed by a larger bank during the banking sector's first consolidation exercise in the country. This experience taught me the importance of being self-confident. In later years, though, I also realised how easily self-confidence could be misconstrued as arrogance depending on the organisation's culture. Self-confidence is built on humility but combined with firm assertiveness. It is also always open to learning.

Grieving and Continuity

One of the most challenging life experiences involves handling the loss of a loved one with whom we have had very strong emotional or filial ties.

One December, my elder brother (the third born) had asked my older brother and I to come to his place one early morning (he lived about ten minutes away). On getting to his house, he came out and blurted out in between tears that Mum had left us that morning. I had never seen my brother cry. She had been terminally ill and had undergone a surgical procedure and had been recuperating at his place.

This loss happened soon after my first return to Nigeria. It certainly took the wind out of me as it all sank in slowly. For that moment, the world around me seemed to have come crashing down, or so it seemed then. I was in quiet shock, thinking about all those wonderful times

I had looked forward to spending with her and the finality of it all. She died in December, just a few days before Christmas, which made it even worse. Things moved quickly after that, as we buried her in January.

Years later, it became clear that I had continued to grieve my mum's loss, often crying myself to sleep quietly. I was over thirty, and the family had moved to Canada.

I had a powerful attachment to my mother, and it wasn't something I could shake off. I recall trying to describe Grandma to my sons, but quickly realising how difficult it was for them to comprehend what she had meant to me.

It just wasn't something I could put together in words. It also took a few years to realise that grieving the way I did was not right, and nor was it fair to those around me with the occasional mood swings that came with it. The true significant memories and emotions I had of her just couldn't be swept away that easily, but as it became more apparent to me, I also had to live up to a father's role to my children. I also recalled an uncle's admonishment to my siblings and I at Mum's service of songs.

As we all tried to maintain the mien of joy at the celebration of her life, as we celebrated her life, it was natural for us to grieve and not suppress our feelings or emotions. The experience also taught me the actual value of life, which is mainly about leaving an impact on the lives of those whom we are privileged to know or encounter in our journey through life.

Money and Fulfilment

One thing I enjoy most about my career choice is learning from the real-life experiences of others in various life and wealth stages. I found wealth brings with it some joys and some burdens too.

Curiously, a common trait of the wealthy as I learnt, however, is the drive to gain more wealth. I had grown up naively believing that the journey to gaining wealth was a finite one and with a clear destination. I was so wrong. The relentless hunger for wealth is often associated with the traits of highly driven and financially successful individuals. The desire for gains drives action. ROI rules most investment decisions outside of the choices of impact investing.

I have met a few people in my journey through life to either shape or moderate this view. Aishat is one of such. We attended the same college many years back, and we had reconnected again about ten years later.

She was running a very successful service business that had gained a good measure of international recognition, though it still operated primarily out of Lagos. I recall once, over lunch, how I had excitedly questioned why she wasn't exploring franchising or other funding arrangements to further expand her business into other commercial cities outside of Lagos. Her response was one I later had to reflect upon profoundly. Despite the promising growth opportunities, she had explained that she was pretty content keeping the business 'small' and 'manageable' and nursed no such ambitions for expansion. She had joked that she hated local air travel anyway but further explained that she felt she needed more time to raise her kids and also wished to ensure that her current service levels in her outlets did not drop, all of which she felt expansion would make more difficult, given the time and commitment that would be required.

Years later, I was having another very personal conversation over drinks in Paris with a very wealthy older friend who lived more in the US. He had recently closed a significant transaction worth a very decent sum and was also planning on disengaging himself from the active involvement in the management of his businesses at the same time. Our conversations had strayed to why wealthy families found it challenging keeping wealth beyond the second generation. Although we were of different cultural backgrounds, we both agreed that it certainly wasn't a challenge limited to any particular culture. We had jointly reeled out several names of huge family businesses that had collapsed through the years.

I had found his own perspective on my country of birth quite insightful. He explained that outside of the rather tricky business operating environment, succession issues faced by patriarchs and matriarchs were sometimes compounded by their polygamous family structures. The assumption that the children of the wealthy would continue in the family's line of business was largely misplaced, as the same children often, after their education in schools in the UK and the US, would opt to explore their passions usually unrelated to the family business. He further explained that the long sentimental hold on such businesses by the patriarchs and matriarchs of these generational businesses which could have been spun off profitably years earlier created its own unique problems.

In all my conversations, I realised no one had attempted to downplay the importance of money. While the motivations ranged from the fears of becoming poor, not having enough to leaving lasting legacies for heirs, money has and would remain relevant. Individuals have different thresholds or limits on the personal sacrifices they will make to gain wealth. However, all seem to seek fulfilment regardless of their wealth state.

As I learned, the hard truth is that the super-wealthy aren't necessarily any happier than those of humbler means. Health and broken-down family relationships were often concerning. With hindsight, the wealthy would say that they would probably have made different choices if given the opportunity to relive their lives again. I learned that pursuing wealth is fair game, but pursuing fulfilment shapes how wealth is pursued and gained.

Passion, People, and Transforming Pain into Purpose

Adaeze Oreh

I started out as a very rambunctious child. As a four-year-old, I was relentlessly correcting my parents, aunts, uncles, younger siblings, and even my headmistress for a wrongly worded sentence or even a wrinkle or rip in their clothes! I was pretty opinionated, and there was no getting me to repress my thoughts.

Over the years, in my early teens, I lost that voice. I became uncertain and anxious about who I was and the role I had to play in my world. As the first of four children, my role as 'Ada' or 'first daughter' was already mapped out for me, but this did not stop me from retreating into shyness as a response to my teenage angst and sudden loss of my early childhood sure-footedness.

As I found myself away from home for the first time arriving at medical school in the red-soiled, temperate climes of scenic, hilly, rural Nsukka, in Nigeria, I became confronted with something much bigger than myself, my fears, and my anxieties. That was the astounding number of people who required various healthcare services but could not afford to get access to them. It consumed me and has since been a cause to which I have committed my time, expertise, and resources; an undertaking that gradually gave me back my voice.

I began my career working in a specialist hospital in Nigeria's Niger Delta region after graduating from the prestigious University of Nigeria, Nsukka, with a degree in medicine. Any day could present anything – from the newly married and hopeful mother-to-be who had recently lost a pregnancy, to the elderly farmer who had a diabetic wound that just would not heal, a nine-year-old with the unrelenting muscle jerks and startling stare of tetanus, a housewife rushed in with her bowels in her hands after a botched surgery by a quack, and victims of gang-war violence with broken teeth and fractured limbs.

During pregnant mother antenatal care clinics, I could see up to 200 women on one clinic day. Women of all tribes and from all walks of life were keen to register their pregnancies because of a state-wide policy that offered free deliveries if registered. First-hand, I saw the power of government policy to drive behaviour change, simply by opening the doors of financial access to everyone.

I thrived in my work and was desperately eager to continue learning more, seizing every opportunity to develop new skills and hone my craft.

Practising medicine, I found enormous fulfilment in my calling as a new mother, wife, and physician when an innocuous-looking lump threw everything sideways. I was diagnosed with a rare type of blood cancer. I was completely blind-sided, terrified, and anxious. With a beautiful infant girl gazing at me with huge, trusting eyes, I resolved to fight the disease with every fibre of my being. This time as a parent and a patient, instead of a physician.

When I recall the intense pain of my bone marrow tests to this day, I wince. Stoic as I could be, I had never felt such heart-wrenching physical agony in my life, but one thing kept me going – the thought of 'after.' For every painful intervention I had to endure, I always held on to the thought of a future where I had conquered the illness and overcome the pain. Day after day, for nearly a year of multiple tests and therapy, that vision of 'after' emboldened by my faith in God was my Uhuru.

During that time of my life, I continued to work, offer my skills, and give other patients care. Stepping out of myself and my pain to help someone else heal offered something even more than professional satisfaction – it offered me hope and a lifeline.

When I was eventually declared cancer-free, I had no doubts about the specialisation I wanted to pursue. I intended to explore healthcare policy and health systems because if there was one thing my gruelling and financially burdensome experience had shown me, it was how catastrophic healthcare expenses could be. With my background and profession, if I was as extended as I was throughout the illness, what hope could there be for the millions who live in poverty or are teetering around it, skirting the possibility of destitution and being tipped over by one medical diagnosis? Therein lay my calling.

However, getting to work in public health policy was not as simple and straightforward as I envisioned. My application gathered dust for months on end. I had interviews with a former Minister of Health and several team members, only to be told there were no positions available. This news was disheartening as all I wanted was to be a public servant, and bring the knowledge, skills, and personal experience I had gained over the years to improve the health of my people.

It was heart-breaking that despite multiple degrees from the University of Nigeria, Imperial College, and then the London School of Hygiene and Tropical Medicine at University College London, it appeared I had to do more to get into that space that would see me in a position to live out this dream of selfless contribution to community healthcare.

With no offer on the horizon, I started a health consultancy firm and an interior design business on the side to keep busy and earn an income. Still, the call to strive for public value unwaveringly beckoned, and I offered my services pro bono as a volunteer with the Federal Ministry of Health. While this did not recompense me in terms of financial income, it was more than rewarding with the exposure, insights, and network I built in the public healthcare space. I got to work closely with other sector professionals on several disease control programmes, community mobilisation initiatives, and various hospital services interventions.

Through this network, I got information about interviews conducted for a US CDC and Federal Ministry of Health project for blood services. Having volunteered for just shy of eight months, hearing this was like a shot in the arm, and I literally raced to the location of the interview.

Barely six hours after they interviewed me, I got the phone call offering me a position to coordinate the Federal Capital Territory project and two neighbouring states. This was the beginning of what has been a challenging but enriching and fulfilling career in public health in Nigeria.

Bringing me to three critical lessons life has taught me:

1. Passion

Each of us has that thing, a driving force that motivates and leads us in specific directions. For me, it has been health and well-being, especially for the most vulnerable, those who can scarcely afford the care they need, and who are most at risk of those illnesses and conditions that can further cement their poverty, take their lives, and leave millions of children orphaned, thus feeding the cycle of poverty, poor education, and disease. I have nurtured this passion, constantly seeking opportunities to gain more insights, and committed my time, expertise, and resources to address this issue professionally and in my community. There is a reason we were born in a particular time and season, and with a specific drive, and therein lies our *raison d'être* – the reason we are here.

2. Transforming Pain to Purpose

When I was diagnosed with Hodgkin's lymphoma as a young mother and physician, it seemed like my world was over. However, confronting this setback with faith and tenacity to overcome it and translating my ordeal to a cause greater than myself has enabled me to grow both personally and professionally. There is a quote I love from Daniel Goleman, the proponent of Emotional Intelligence.

"Self-absorption in all its forms kills empathy, let alone compassion. When we focus on ourselves, our world contracts as our problems and preoccupations loom large. But when we focus on others, our world expands. Our own problems drift to the periphery of the mind and so seem smaller, and we increase our capacity for connection – or compassionate action."

I have strived to take my personal pain and transform it into a life of purpose in public service, a career that is not really about me, but about the people I serve through my work.

3. Connection and the Importance of People

Over the years, I have learned the power of what I can loosely refer to as connections or connectedness. By this, I do not mean the high-brow nepotistic type of connection, that worn Nigerian cliché. Instead, the link I refer to is that social kinship or interconnectedness that occurs when people work together towards a common goal rooted in the growth and strengthening of the community. That affinity arises when our gifts, knowledge, and skills are brought together in unity and not in competition, and in so doing, we create a symphony of purposeful living. That is the connection that is incredibly powerful and can transform communities and revolutionise nations.

I have seen this play out in the nearly two decades I have spent in my career. Having doors of opportunity opened for me in many unlikely places, being encouraged by a community of people who are deeply committed to the common good and not absorbed or motivated by personal gain. However, to harness the power of connectedness, one must continually strive to better oneself, improve, and share one's knowledge, skills, and time to add value. It is that perception of value that attracts opportunities.

To live fully and richly requires that we live for a higher purpose than purely to survive. To thrive in whatever space or wherever we find ourselves, we must have a why, a purpose, a higher calling. The COVID-19 pandemic brought with it a near-constant and determinedly unyielding barrage of uncertainty, grief, suffering, and loss for so many. By holding on firmly to our reasons for being, we can peer through these dark moments, prise open the cracks of hope, part the dark curtains of hopelessness, focus, and see the light.

As Maya Angelou says,

"My mission in life is not merely to survive, but to thrive; and to do so with some passion, some compassion, some humour, and some style."

That, too, is my mission.

Never Underestimate Any Tasks That Are Assigned to You

Junjuan He

I genuinely believe that every single job, regardless of its scale, amount, or self-defined importance, is worth the experience in the business world.

My work ethic is such that I won't say no to a single task or request from a colleague or manager. The only time I would refuse is if the task were unnecessary or would harm the company in some way.

I would complete any task, even if it weren't glamorous or exciting. I believe that every experience is worth it, and you will get your reward for the experience in your life eventually, so I will try my best to figure out a very efficient way to perform it. I have benefited so much over my career with this firm belief, so I want to share my story with you all today. I hope it can help you.

At the beginning of my career, I had always been ambitious. I was determined that I would be consistent in making a significant impact on the organisation, very much like a CEO. Some would say, even back then, I had a C-suite executive's mindset and the drive to be a leader.

I have always placed a lot of value on academic qualifications. Even though I worked very hard to polish the professional skills required for my role, it was enhanced by acquiring professional certifications to demonstrate my expertise. I was also very picky about the tasks they assigned me because I was diligent about not being underutilised. I wanted to be a solid contributor to the organisation.

Whenever my boss assigned me a task, job, or assignment I felt was not significant enough, such as preparing some introductory presentation or conducting some research on a particular topic, I would make every single possible excuse to avoid taking on that responsibility. I would usually appeal to my boss using the excuse that I felt I had more to offer and that my skills would be better used elsewhere.

In the beginning, my boss tried to persuade me that every single job, regardless of its scale, counts in professional life. But after a few discussions with me, luckily or unluckily, my boss was kind enough to show understanding about my thoughts and was equally forgiving of what I would now look at as my arrogance. He mentioned he was evaluating my potential and wanted me to grow, so he assigned most of the routine tasks to another team member, who incidentally was my peer and didn't seem to mind taking care of those other tasks, projects, and assignments I had considered menial. And he also assigned me a few large, meaningful, and cross-functional projects.

After a period, my peer became more and more familiar with the operation of the business. While he became more knowledgeable about various parts of our operation, my knowledge of the operation was going in the other direction. That difference in our skill set became even more apparent because, at some point, our team was preparing a vast project whose scale and cost was going to make some considerable differences to the company's bottom line.

Guess what? They promoted my colleague to lead the project. To further emphasise how well he had benefited from his knowledge of the business, they promoted him again to a more senior position after successfully completing the project.

I encountered some challenges in the projects they assigned me because I was not familiar with all the operations, especially in the areas where I was assigned, but refused to become familiar with them. I thought those small dots were not essential, but I forgot that without every single small dot, you cannot form lines and areas. As a result, some projects were not as successful as I expected.

I was shocked at this turn of events because I saw things differently. I thought I was working very hard on projects that were important to the business. At the same time, I was polishing my knowledge of the business, even on the weekends, and diligently working on the tasks that I thought were important.

However, what I was missing was the bigger picture, simply because I had been too focused on what I imagined being the important tasks. In doing so, I not only starved myself of the opportunity to understand the business better, but I also became less valuable and too inflexible because my lack of knowledge limited the opportunities I was given to expand.

This failure and setback made me realise never to pick and choose a task, since every effort is worth it in the future, and success is about incremental gain rather than a single big project. All those so-called small and non-eye-catching tasks are foundations for our career path, especially in the early stages. Without a solid foundation, it isn't easy to build a great building.

From then on, I decided that I would never make the excuse to be picky about tasks unless it was entirely useless. I discussed this with my manager and shared my changed mindset towards the job with him. He showed lots of understandings and happiness about the positive change in me.

I worked hard on every single task that was part of my responsibilities, regardless of scale. My hard-working and responsible attitude soon earned me an excellent reputation across the company and high evaluations from people around me, including the management. Soon, people in my team or on projects took me more seriously because I was not only knowledgeable about the operation but was also responsible and accountable. Gradually, I was assigned other critical projects in the company and promoted as the senior manager in a very short space of time because I had successfully delivered all the projects I was assigned.

I had learned and grew a lot from these experiences; that we should be responsible and accountable not just for the big scale projects but also on the day-to-day routine, since our reputations and foundations are built on it. I am very appreciative of my manager for being patient and allowing me the space to grow by myself, instead of giving harsh advice. He has been an excellent model for me as a leader, showing that sometimes people need time to think and grow at their pace.

As a leader today, I am trying my best efforts to create the environment and time to allow my team members to grow.

Do What Makes You Feel Alive

Nina Bressler

To understand my story, you need to understand the stories of my family and of my people that I carry with me. My story is of an adventure in search of a life. Because of this story, I have come to build a life where my purpose is to feel alive, every day, in all that I do. To understand my commitment to my purpose, you must understand the story that swallowed me up when I was born, the duty that it brought with it, and the path that it has led me to follow.

Both my parents were born in Leningrad before the start of the Second World War. My mother was four years old, my father six, when the Nazi troops blockaded Leningrad in September 1941. The Siege of Leningrad lasted 872 days and was one of the longest in history and resulted in the intentional genocide of the city's civilian population. They both have memories of the terror, of the doom, of starvation, and escape. One of my mother's earliest memories was being loaded into a transport that would evacuate women and children out of Leningrad across a frozen Lake Ladoga, on what was known as the Road of Life. As winter cold set in on a starving Leningrad, the lake froze and became an avenue for a few lucky citizens to escape the siege of their beloved city. As they crossed the lake, my mother and grandmother watched from their transport as the other transport travelling alongside theirs fell through the ice; no one survived. The Road of Life allowed both my parents to escape a siege that led to the death of over one million citizens of Leningrad. They were the lucky ones; their luck is my luck.

After the war, the citizens of Leningrad, while healing from the collective trauma of war, stepped into the dark night of the post-war Soviet Union. In the shadows of repression and fear, people found their humanity in music, art, writing, in laughter. The opportunity to freely explore what makes you feel alive is a luxury; in the shadow of repression, the light it brings into your life is coveted. A person has to push through the edge of the fear to find the light, and my mother did just that when she left the Soviet Union with my grandmother and brother. Again, luck was with her – Russian Jews had an opportunity to emigrate to Israel in the late seventies. Once you were across the Iron Curtain, many families became refugees and found their way to societies they saw as beacons of hope. The United States, Canada,

Australia, and other countries opened their arms to the people living under a totalitarian regime. My father was meant to follow within two years, but the Soviet war with Afghanistan resulted in the borders being closed, and his journey to the West took nine more years.

 My mother's crossing took her through Vienna, where as a refugee she waited for asylum in the United States with my brother and grandmother. It was a difficult time. To move through the guilt of leaving their homeland, of leaving their family, and the uncertainty of life in the West, they had to find moments when they could truly feel alive, like purchasing a standing ticket to the Vienna Opera or a discounted entrance to the Albertina. As they discovered freedom and a fresh way of being in the world, my mother found out that she was pregnant with me. People told her she was crazy, as a forty-two-year-old woman, as a refugee who needed to establish a new life, as someone with very little English, even to consider having the baby. Yet, despite the odds, she gave me life. I was born in Vienna and joined my mother, brother and grandmother on their voyage to the United States.

My childhood in America allowed me to explore and follow my passions. I grew up in many cultures –

Russian, Bostonian, equestrian, rock'n'roll, and more. The innate adaptability and curiosity that each of us is born with gave me the ability to merge into each of my environments, absorbing the beliefs and thoughts of those around me. I could witness my mother's hunger for life as she pursued a stable home for us in Boston. My brother, sixteen years older than me, playing the role of "man of the house" in our matriarchy, was eager to make sense of the world through the lens of mathematics and completed his PhD at the Massachusetts Institute of Technology. So rich and varied was the story of the people around me. I wanted to experience it ALL, to know and understand them, see the beauty of life through their eyes. So, as you can see, the story that I was born into was one of luck, and with that came an unspoken sense of duty.

The sense of duty one feels to their family's legacy can be both an enabler and a hindrance. It had a constricting power over me in my formative years, a power against which I rebelled. In that rebellion, I pursued what brought me joy, even when I perceived it as being outside my family's expectations: horses, music, and art were my rebellion against duty; what I perceived as rebellion brought with it a lack of harmony. In my mind and because of the spoken or unspoken messages from my family and cultural environment, I often perceived that I was not fulfilling the expectations of my parents, of the other respected voices in my life, and felt judgement and pressure. I dealt with that by pushing against those perceived boundaries even more.

As I matured, I realised that sense of duty had actually enabled me. I have translated that sense of duty into my commitment to life with few boundaries. The freedom to explore and create is what feeds me, makes me feel alive, and is my greatest power. I now understand that it is my duty to my legacy to live. I could see how judgement can make us hide and repress ourselves. It takes a mental tenacity and presence in every moment not to give in to these doubts, and that only comes with practice. With that practice, I have learned to find my greatest power and energy when immersed in something that fascinates me and frees me from others' expectations. I ground my expectations in my sense of duty to myself and my legacy.

Do What Makes You Feel Alive

What makes me feel alive? To answer this, I took a journey into my body and mind, an expedition of curiosity where I became fascinated with observing myself and the energy within me. I am a firm believer that to live, we must each go on this journey honestly. It will be different for each of us, but it is the path to freedom. The discoveries I have made on this journey are no permanent truths; they develop and change over time, but they always integrate what came before them.

This is what I discovered: I am blessed with the power to go deep, and it is my duty to use it, to be present wholeheartedly in all that I do with passion and interest. I am insatiably hungry to see, feel and experience, and pass along what I've learned. It is my duty to feed this hunger, to bring this "aliveness" to all that I do. This aliveness can be powerful and overwhelming for others, sometimes causing strong and unintentional reactions. People are provoked when it pokes at their fears. When released in a fertile environment, it can catalyse change and transformation. So daily I recommit myself to the story I was born into: Do What Makes You Feel Alive.

From that starting point, one must truly understand what practises bring with them aliveness. For me, it is to have a healthy outlet for my strength and tenacity, to push experiences to the edge without being reckless, experience intensity without aggression. To say no to living in a disempowered state. To say yes, express myself how I want to run at full throttle when that is my desire.

To choose anything else is repression. As I know from my own experiences and those of my ancestors, repression brings on anxiety or depression and a fear of feeling anything at all. To release myself, I must dive beneath the surface and play in those spaces where I can trust the environment and relinquish control. As I release my need to control, my vitality comes to the surface. I allow myself to experience the full spectrum of emotions from sadness to joy, and appreciate that every emotion is a sign that I am alive and all of life is beautiful.

Learning about the creative and intellectual pursuits of others allows me to experience the light of their aliveness. It is an invitation to join them in living. I always say yes to such an invitation. Yes, to sharing a story, sharing a laugh, sharing a struggle, or sharing in someone else's curiosity. They are beautiful and joyous exchanges, even when the content is not always happy. This connection brings us energy.

Giving myself to another brings me the greatest sense of aliveness. That means trusting another with my feelings, body, and energy – whether it is my horse, partner, family, friends, or colleagues. My love of horses has been a life journey in developing my awareness of how vital this trust and release of control is for me. I fell in love with horses from the age of eight and did everything I could to work with them. From the age of ten, I would work at the stables every weekend and all summer for opportunities to ride and be with horses. I thought that this experience of aliveness was something I could only find on the back of a horse for most of my life. To trust a 600kg animal to carry you, to feel your deepest fears and

to push you to expand your wholehearted leadership past the edge of what you thought possible is a beautiful experience. I crave it daily and have committed myself to it fully for the past thirty-three years. Many of the decisions in my life and motivations have come from my hunger for that experience.

Today, that need is fulfilled with my horse, Cherry Bomb, with whom I have a beautiful trust under saddle, in the woods, over a jump, or just grooming her in her stall. But, in my deep commitment to being with horses, there used to be an underlying fear that held me back, a fear that I could not find that same experience of joy, trust and aliveness elsewhere in life.

This limiting belief was washed away when I was fortunate to have my career journey lead me to join a tribe of Curious Minds. These Curious Minds are the teams I work with at Novartis: my 100,000-plus peers and colleagues who surprise me daily with their incredible commitment to bettering the world by reimagining medicine. The people outside my organisation who inspire me and are partners or thought leaders advocate for a view that passionate exploration and unfettered curiosity are the ultimate energy source for feeling alive. In putting this work into focus, in diving deep into it, I've found the people with whom I could feel the most alive. This was a eureka moment for me that the same experience I had on the back of a horse could also be had in the experience of co-creating impact and exploring the world together with others. This revelation seems like such an obvious truth, but it took me almost forty years to become conscious of how important this truth is in my life.

The journey to this lesson has been a long one; it started in the story that I was born into and emerged for me only when I found my tribe of co-explorers when I stopped repressing my energy, when I began to trust my aliveness, and when I saw that it was my duty to my legacy to do so. I have learned the lesson that when we come together with others around a shared purpose, we can unlock our greatest potential. It is our shared duty as humans to ensure that all people have the opportunity to *Do What Makes Us Feel Alive*.

So, I want to share the lesson I learned: never underestimate any task assigned to you or under your responsibilities. Please embrace it with excitement, since it will reward you for your efforts and the time you spent. Remember: life is like a box of chocolates; you never know what you're going to get!

Work-Life Balance is a Myth

Amelia Samai-Nicome

At the age of twenty-six, I became a young female executive. At the time, I had no significant responsibilities in my personal life, and the time which the job required me to dedicate towards it was not a burden; it was understandable. After all, this was in pursuit of the furtherance of my career. Late evenings and working weekends were not an issue, and I was the go-to person if they needed it. I should mention that the commute one way to this job was anywhere between one and a half to two hours.

After just a few years, my personal life situation changed. At twenty-eight, I got married, and shortly after that, my husband and I welcomed our first son. Although I received three months of maternity leave, I took only one month off; after all, I needed to get back to my job.

In hindsight, I can admit that I underestimated the amount of time and work required to care adequately for a child and a family. It took me a while to make the mental shift necessary, as I believed it was easy enough to make a trade-off between my son and my job, as my son was very well taken care of by his great-grandmother and grandmother, both of whom waited on him and catered to his every need.

My husband and I both needed to maintain our jobs, so it meant we worked all day and could spend evenings with our son. Initially, we thought this to be an adequate amount of time to facilitate our son. However, to facilitate evenings, it meant that I could no longer work late evenings. So, without realising it, the balancing act began.

As our son became older, it was increasingly difficult to work weekends; since anyone who is a dedicated parent knows, three hours an evening with your child doesn't cut it. Besides this, as life stays true to form, it threw a few curvesballs my way.

Within the first year of my son's life, his great-grandmother died, and his grandmother was facing some health challenges. The support system that allowed me to "balance" being a very involved parent while pursuing my career was now non-existent. There was barely any time to mourn as life and the demands of work stop for no one.

This was one of those points in life where tough decisions had to be made. You would think it would be easy enough to place our son in day care and move on with our daily lives. After all, there are millions of other parents who do this. However, our son was a bit of a miracle baby. The doctors gave him less than a 50% chance of being carried to full term and being born unaffected, given I experienced some complications with his pregnancy. Yet he beat the odds and was here with us, and I could not find it within myself to leave his care to chance. This was a major element or shift that weighed heavily into the balancing act.

Comparatively, my job was deemed more secure than my husband's, and I made a higher salary, so we decided my husband would become a stay-at-home dad for our son just until he started school. This change came with many adjustments. First, we had to adjust our way of life, as we moved from two incomes to one. Things as simple as buying takeout were now switched to more home cooking. We had to accept we would be on a stricter budget.

Anyone who moves from being a working parent to being a stay-at-home parent has their own transition to go through, and this was no different for my husband. There were days he was great, and then days when he needed more support to adjust to his new role in our family.

Another curveball. We found out that I was pregnant with our second son three months into the pregnancy. Some months after his arrival, I went through a near-death experience, where I was hospitalised for about two weeks. This was another shift in my balancing act. Within this ordeal, by the time I got into the hospital, the doctors couldn't find my pulse, although I was awake. I'm not sure how, but I called my mother and told her about my situation. I spoke to my husband, and I made my peace with God before going into surgery. I was sure I wouldn't be coming out, and I had two boys aged five years and nine months old whom I would probably never see again, nor be around to raise.

I promise you my job was not my focus. It was unfortunate that it took a near-death experience to bring me to my senses and adjust my work-life balance perspective. Up to that point, my work and career had taken centre stage over my family.

After my stay in the hospital, I was sent home to recover, and this in itself was very difficult to manage. There were nights I swore I would not make it through, and I could not walk without support. My husband, however, nursed me back to health, and after what seemed like a lifetime of two months, I was allowed to return to work with adjusted hours.

In comes another shift in perspective. Within the job, they placed me in a programme to be trained and promoted as the head of the organisation. I was flattered, and I believe my ego got the best of me. Rather than turn it down because of my responsibilities at home and health issues, I took the opportunity, much to the neglect of my family. I was one person who was having a hard time adjusting my perspective and learning my lessons. I chased that elusive work-life balance or perfect state. I was sure after they promoted me, I could manage the demands more effectively once I got the staff I needed.

It got so demanding that many weekends I would bring the kids into the office with me so that I could see them while I worked. Yes, see them. Because, given the commute, most mornings I left before they got up, and they were asleep or up for an hour when I got home. I couldn't do it anymore, as having the kids on the road at the weekends while their friends were going to the beach or park wasn't fair to them. In addition to which the job for which I was sacrificing my family, was no longer being offered to me. I needed to make a decision and commit to it. I left the job.

My work-life conundrum continued until I learned a few things. I first had to accept my changing circumstances. It is easy to wait and hope for things to return to normal, but once a change occurred, I needed to do my best to adjust rather than refuse to acknowledge my change or move out of my comfort zone.

I had to come to terms with the fact that *I could not have it all.* Something that I was not willing to admit to myself. Many people may disagree with me, but a healthy work-life balance allows us to accept this. With each changing circumstance, my priority changed, and what I deemed balanced previously was now out of balance because of the change in my circumstance and perspective. We must be willing to sacrifice something to achieve a work-life balance. But when we prioritise, we consciously determine those things to which we must tend. When we find a way to give time to the priorities in our life, we believe that we have achieved a work-life balance. In reality, the scales may be well out of balance, but if the ratio gives us a sense that the essential areas of our lives are being given adequate attention, we can keep fooling ourselves into thinking that we have achieved work-life balance.

I had to become comfortable saying no, even to tip the scales in the right direction. One of the significant sources of my work-life disequilibrium was because somewhere in the back of my head, I thought I needed to say yes and facilitate every request that came my way.

It took me a long time to adjust my thinking and understand that saying no didn't make me a selfish person. It just meant that I needed to tend to my own requests before helping others with theirs.

To achieve work-life balance, I realised I could not allow another person's agenda to take precedence over mine and dictate what I should view as important. Other individuals will guilt you into believing that there is something wrong with your priorities if they do not coincide with their needs.

Honestly, it stopped mattering to me some time ago if my seniors got upset because I needed to take off work to tend to an issue at home. I was comfortable that I gave above and beyond what they required of me for the job. My need to be more involved with matters at home was and still is used in bypassing me for opportunities within my career. Honestly, I will tell anyone, go ahead and bypass me. Someone looking for an excuse not to give you an opportunity will find one, no matter what. If being very involved and responsible for my family is that, I wish them all the best. In balancing work-life responsibilities, you have to deliver on the commitments made. So as long as I have met my commitments to my job, I must equally find the time to meet the commitments made to my family.

My kids didn't ask to be brought into this world, and my husband and I didn't bring them here to neglect them. My husband has been by my side through thick and thin; how could I sacrifice his needs to facilitate that of a company who would happily replace me the next day if something happened to me?

I would tell anyone never to feel guilty or allow themselves to be guilted for caring about their family. Even though a company understands that you may be a star performer who adds value beyond compare, a company can replace you at the drop of a hat. Don't think for a second that if a company's strategic direction changes and you no longer suit its needs, they won't leave you behind.

I would encourage everyone to use vacation benefits for a holiday! For too many years, my holidays have been me being partially present on family holidays while always needing one minute to reply to an email. My behaviour could easily encourage poor performance and unnecessary dependability in others within the workplace. If you aim to achieve a high level of work-life balance, then be willing to delegate to others. Be happy to train someone to take over your portfolio so that you can get that needed break from work.

Concerning COVID-19, one of the most significant shifts in work-life balance history ever, there are a few things I would say:

1. As long as you are doing your best for your family and your job, your absolute best, then you are doing well, so give yourself credit for it. Don't feel guilty for not having it all under control.
2. For those of us who were thrown into work from home and homeschooling, getting up even one hour earlier to deal with the matters at work that require your heaviest concentration is worth investing in. Or if you work better at night, then take an extra hour after the kids are in bed.
3. Keep your routine. If you would usually have commute times, get up at the same times and use

the time to read or develop yourself. Self-care is vital in maintaining a work-life balance. If you break down, the whole system breaks down. Invest in exercise routines or whatever calms your spirit, but connect with yourself often, as that is the only way to know if you are handling the balancing act well or if you need to readjust your scales.

4. Please remember to be patient with your co-workers and your kids. Everyone is stressed out right now.

5. Be kind to yourself, as we don't all get it right the first time, and there's no need to, as long as we learn and grow from our experiences. Commit to doing better once you learn new things and you will realise you can do better in your own time.

6. If your current work-life scales aren't working because you are still feeling unfulfilled, do some shifting, but try to maintain objectivity.

7. I've learned that what works for me won't necessarily work for you, so don't judge or allow others to weigh in too heavily on your decisions. You need to know what is right for you, your career, and your family. Only you will know what that entails.

Your version of work-life balance will be uniquely yours. Whatever leaves you feeling fulfilled and content, that you have done your best to adequately tend to your responsibilities, that's what it's all about.

Nurture What is Most Important

Shervonne Johnson

One of the greatest lessons I have learned in life is that learning can happen anytime, in any place, and may come from anyone. For example, learning may happen in a classroom, at church, in a cubicle at work, or even on or at someone's deathbed. As for sources of learning, we may learn from a child, an older person, in an argument, during a quiet moment, from people we love, people we dislike (or who dislike us), when times are easy, or when times are hard.

For my contribution, I share some of the lessons I have learned in life that have affected who I am today, and that may prove helpful to others as one navigates life.

L1: The most important voice you can hear is your own – nurture your inner voice, but do not replace it

Growing up in the Bahamas, one does not have to look far to find a powerful maternal presence 'guiding you.' Matriarchal societies are responsible for many successful leaders all over the "for the doors that never opened... I am coming to buy the entire building!" world. Why? They are wonderful nurturers. They somehow seem to get the best out of us by example, fear, or threats not to fail and how we had better do our best.

However, in their nurturing, sometimes we end up hearing their dreams, hopes, and fears in our minds. Some love and nurture us unconditionally. Some of their actions are our presumed obligation, and some are just doing (healthily or unhealthily) what they learned along the way. In my family, I had aunts, grandmothers, neighbours, colleagues, and more who, without hesitation, would give you their opinion on whom you should date, what you should eat, what to do with your money, hair, what careers to pursue, and whether or not to have children; all completely unsolicited.

Life has taught me that most of this 'direction' came from a place of love. However, I also believe that this can delay us in forming or solidifying our own thoughts and values. I believe strongly in being grounded; however, I also believe that this should only be a foundation. We must take all that is poured into us and find our own voice. When we find our voice, it helps us have more confidence, innate drive, and motivation. We seek external validation less because it is all coming from inside. We hear our soul speaking versus the pressure to be what everyone else thinks we should be.

L2: Ensure your time investments align with who and what you care about

Time is something you can never replace once it is gone. There are many activities throughout our lives to which we will dedicate our time. Time spent with family, maintaining one's health, and career is important. Time spent on accomplishing one's dreams is essential, as is time spent with friends.

From the time we are born, we start using time. I like to think of life in decades. As it relates to time, I like to think about different decades of our life. We were either in control of how we spent our time, or someone else determined how we spent our time. The older we get (hopefully), the more autonomy we have to decide how and where we spend our time.

Many people over the years have said they admired my ability to somehow do so much with my time. I am a mom, a professional, a bubbly extroverted socialite, a great networker, churchgoer, exerciser, avid follower of world news and trends, involved in community service and organisations – the list goes on.

While all of this is true, what I would share is that being involved also means your time is pulled in many directions, and at the same time. Sometimes it is exhilarating, and other times it is draining. I want to focus on the latter. Whenever I have felt drained, I found a direct correlation to me not mastering time. In particular, I found that I was giving time to people and activities that I did not most care about and as a result, it left me feeling guilty about not giving my time to persons or activities that fed my soul!

Throughout my career, I cannot tabulate the number of hours I have spent within my employers' walls (many times doing the work of others who did not carry their weight or ever say thank you). Over the decades of my life, I cannot count the hours I have spent around energy vampires, 'haters', and, to be frank, just people I did not care for, or people who did not mean me well. I have spent time on activities that did not add to my home life, my happiness or develop my talents: my bottom line – time accountability.

I believe it is important only to do and spend time on things that bring you joy. That does not mean relationships, activities, or careers will not be challenging, but if it is something or someone you genuinely care about, you will never regret such time spent. These moments in life feed a special part of our souls.

Ensure that your time investment aligns with who and what you care about. You cannot say you love to garden, but never plant or water one tree. You cannot say family is important to you, but never spend time with your loved ones over all your other activities. You cannot say your career is essential to you, yet spend no time or money improving your skills and performance. You cannot say children are only children once, but do not carve out time from work or social life to spend quality time with them.

Our actions must match our words when it comes to time because once it is gone, it is gone. My suggestion, every year, is to identify two big things you would like to accomplish in one area of your life. Detail specific things that must happen for you to accomplish this goal and dedicate time for these little milestones. Every month, rotate the different people in your life (we all have different circles of love and energy), and make a targeted effort to do something with each group.

Every week, if you have children, decide what will be 'that thing', 'that night', 'that show' or 'that dish' that you are going to share just with your kids. If you have a partner, though they may be understanding, ensure that you look that person in the eye almost every day and engage with them on a personal level. It's funny how as time passes, detachment occurs. When you measure your 'lost time,' ensure you spent it attached and enjoying who you love and what you care about. It is very sustaining.

L3: Ask to be at the table – do not wait to be asked

Because of race, gender, school, or other affiliations, as a professional, one may find oneself in a room with others who make you feel 'different'. Unfortunately, the world we live in sometimes makes being 'different' a bad thing. However, diversity is the key, and the world is appreciating this more and more.

Until the world catches up, you must remain 'the Captain of your Fate'. You cannot allow anyone else to determine when you will be present. When you are present, you must make it count. As a woman, foreigner (at times) and person of colour, I have been the one who was 'different'. Through wonderful mentorships that ignored such differences, I learned not to focus on the exterior, but more on what I had to contribute. Exclusion of others is a learnt behaviour. Many times, the person committing the offence is not aware of their discriminatory and harmful behaviour.

As a result, you are most responsible for making your presence felt and showing that you have something to contribute. Many biases are unintentional. Many people gravitate to what they are familiar with. If you make the first move and show that you and those around you may have similarities, you are competent. You have something of value to add or possible common interests, which makes it easier for any imaginary walls to come down.

Having said that, I believe you should always know why you are where you are, what you hope to get out of the experience, and not be intimated by what surrounds you. Just be confident enough to either take a seat at the table or ask to join the meeting. Over my career, I would do things such as look at someone in the contact list and see that they were very senior in the company; I would just call them and ask them a question about what I wanted to know. They got to know who I was, and eventually, instead of asking to be at the table, I was asked to join.

As a professional, outside of your talent, exposure to strategic projects, change initiatives, new product and service rollouts, major regulatory breaches, complex internal, and external audits, and others outside the norm activities are great opportunities to professionally really grow. Do not miss out on such opportunities, because you are waiting to be asked. Ask to take part, say what type of projects interest you, embed it in your goal setting and performance management process.

If where you work has women, ethic or interest-based initiatives, then take part and use these opportunities to help improve your chances of being at the table! Do not let them forget you.

L4: Having an ally is a powerful thing

*"There is at least one thing worse than fighting with allies
– and that is to fight without them."*
Sir Winston Churchill –
Former British Prime Minister

Being independent is a beautiful thing. Accomplishing things all on one's own is an empowering thing. However, having an ally is a practical thing. There are communities and societies in every institution in our lives. In churches, schools, at work, within families and other organisations, there is an energy that connects or separates us. During my career and in my personal life, having allies undoubtedly helped me navigate difficult situations more smoothly. Your allies ideally should have a myriad of characteristics to make them an effective ally. Mine had power, money, status, social standing, beauty, possessed a valuable network, and were loving, caring, dedicated, loyal, influential, feared, respected, and in demand.

I used my allies wisely and always showed my gratitude. This kept my access to them always open. Sometimes it was a look, sometimes a call, a conversation over dinner, an email or even an indirect request. I also protected my allies as they were worth more than precious stones to me. Each time I used my allies versus fighting alone, it was a more positive outcome. Build a diverse network of allies and use this network to work smarter rather than harder.

My allies also were a source of 'heads up' before something terrible happened or the inside scope when something controversial happened. Or even a head start to an opportunity before it was even publicly known. My advice is to develop a global and local network of allies who represent a cross-section of your life's purposes.

L5: You cannot pour from an empty cup

Burnout is so real. The human body and spirit are not a machine; they must be fed and nourished. I have experienced various forms of burnout throughout my career. Thank goodness I am past that point in my life, though! I now have tremendous respect for balance and even greater respect for listening to the signs my mind, body, and soul are sending me. What does burnout look like, how does it feel? Low energy, weight gain (especially in the mid-section), a drop in interest in things you love, broken sleep patterns, just to name a few.

You can have the biggest heart and excellent drive in the world, but if you do not slow down and recharge soon, you will be no good to anyone else. The sad thing with burnout is that the people who love you want and deserve your presence. You have nothing leftover to enjoy them.

Even worse is when they celebrate you and show you love, but you do not even realise it because you are just drained. I have experienced all of the above.

Now I make me-time a crucial part of any relationship. Sometimes I drive to the beach during my workday and just listen to silly jokes. I come home and make it a point to ask my daughter how was her day or what is going on with her friends (or I just need to walk in the door, and she is just telling me non-stop).

I take vacations by myself and with people who are good travel partners only! I make it a point to know the staff at my favourite restaurants because they are really my escape, my therapists (they just do not know)! I live in one of the most beautiful places on earth. I try to start as many mornings as possible by the beach. Something about being by the ocean prepares me for any day.

Make Diversity Your Advantage

Susana Ecclestone

"Kites rise highest against the wind, not with it."
Sir Winston Churchill –
Former British Prime Minister

"She stood in the storm,
and when the wind did not blow her way,
she adjusted her sails."
Elizabeth Edwards –
American attorney and author

It would have been difficult to expect what life would be like, considering the easy ride I had as a child. Somehow, I find a loving, easy childhood to blame for the lack of tools that I needed to survive in my adult life. However, I cannot but wonder if my carefree childhood somehow prepared me for the hurdles to come, creating a solid foundation of character building and self-confidence.

In my case, it can be described as having a peaceful environment of loving parents, growing up unaware of any family conflicts, although this does not mean they did not exist. I only just found out of some of these later on in life, as most adults start discovering skeletons in anyone's closet, but which had been safely put away until I was older and more able to understand.

I am conscious there are many more still uncovered, but I am not sure I am too curious about those. It would be helpful to have information to fill specific gaps and perhaps a relatively obscure family tree.

I grew up hearing the typical stories of Italian relatives coming to Argentina on boats in the 1900s and working hard to survive, having huge family fights that meant fortunes were lost, and other random details. These made the stories a bit more colourful, but lacked evidence, photos, or any other information to dig any further.

My grandmother was the first of six children to be born in Argentina. Her older sister was born on the Aquila, that arrived in the port of Buenos Aires in 1890.

My father grew up in a typical middle-class family in Argentina, from what could have been a very comfortable upper-class upbringing. Still, again, muddled stories of multiple fortunes lost. Family fights left only enough to live in 1940's Argentina, a very non-European country mostly populated by Europeans that had arrived at the beginning of the war and would continue arriving for many years more.

At the time, Argentina was sophisticated, wealthy, and was known as the "Granero del Mundo" (the barn that fed the world), being the leading exporter of grain to the post-WWII European countries that were struggling.

My mother grew up in extreme poverty in the centre of Argentina with many brothers and sisters, most of whom I never met, together with cousins and other relatives whose stories are purposely vague thanks to my mother, who always kept that part of her life packed away from us. I think I inherited this compartmentalisation system, storing memories in virtual boxes.

I cannot but wonder where most of my more distant relatives are or who they were, but at the same time, it is part of the family folklore that you just did not know and did not ask too much.

As you get older, you want to pass these stories onto your children, but you realise you had very little, and they lose so much history along the way.

Only when I raised my own children did I understand the power of experience, demanding situations, and struggles to form a young person and prepare them for the future. It may sound harsh, but adversity seems to be the foundation of exceptional individuals and resilience the key to success.

> "It's your reaction to adversity, not adversity itself, that determines how your life's story will develop."
> Dieter F. Uchtdorf –
> German religious leader

I often wonder what would have happened or how things would have turned out if I didn't have those unique personal experiences, but only briefly and as part of a retrospection and self-awareness exercise.

Going back in time is only useful if there is a lesson to be learned. Instead, I made a conscious decision to follow the path of "moving forward," knowing that I have accumulated a few learning tools to fight new battles.

It is difficult to avoid the "what ifs," but I cannot resist looking back and wonder: what if I had not left Argentina in 2001 and moved to NY right before the Twin Towers were attacked? What if I had stayed in the US instead of moving to the UK? What if I had continued teaching instead of moving into healthcare? What if I had stayed in Argentina or had moved to the US in 1988, as I originally had planned? What if...?

Life was uncomplicated as a child, loving family, easy life, hard-working parents with a lack of luxuries: exotic holidays or international travel were not even on the cards for any of us, and it seemed natural not to expect them either. A few additional comforts, a country house, some local beach holidays, what we would now call 'staycations,' resulted from lots of sacrifices and saving every penny.

Nothing came easy for my mother, who was raised by a very forward-thinking liberal mother who knew her children's future lay very far away from their town and sent them all to the big city as soon as they could make a living on their own. She expected nothing from them, but all looked after her even when travelling was not so affordable, adored her deeply, and distances seemed farther. My grandmother was a woman who never complained, had a very harsh life and worked non-stop but knew how to give her children wings.

My father grew up in an upper-middle-class environment with few financial worries but was living in an unsettled country, where one economic and political disaster after another led to just a comfortable life and not much more. Starting in 1930 with the first military coup that deposed Hipólito Yrigoyen, the rest of the Argentine political history is a roller coaster of coups and military regimes where most people lost more and more of not only savings and investments, but also social status and influence.

In 1976, the military coup that deposed Maria Estela Martinez de Perón lasted for eight years. This event had a significant impact on my life, since living under a military regime dictates most of what you do and how you do it.

During these years, political activists disappeared (known as Los Desaparecidos), and life was about what you did not discuss in public. Although I was young, I definitely feel this also significantly affected the way I live today. There was always a great sense of duty and responsibility to God, having attended Catholic schools all my life, to the motherland, and the family. It was not discussed, debated or spoken, but it was there.

I left Argentina in the middle of a terrible economic depression and started a journey I never planned.

Living abroad was everything few people talk about: the sudden lack of family, friends and a support networks, the poor communication tools of the time and the sometimes incredibly substantial cultural gap, and subtle and sometimes not-so-subtle discrimination. So many other challenges kept piling onto my resilience.

The 9/11 attacks created a situation that can be measured only now in the negative impact it has had on the world. The towers keep falling every day; the impact and damage is greater and greater, and has brought out the worst in some governments and only sometimes the best in individuals.

I feel that this tragedy somehow marked my life, although only indirectly. It changed what I assumed my future would be like, and it triggered a chain of events that took me to where I am today, leading me to leave America and come to England. I wanted a lot more exposure to the real world for my children, and America closes in on you to the point where you lose a worldwide perspective of reality.

Life has taught me you not only make lemonade out of lemons, but you also diversify the production. You create, reinvent and regroup many times over and as much as needed. It is a tough road but necessary if you want to grow as a person and as a professional.

Life has also taught me that one life is not enough. Every time you need to start over, you reinvent yourself and hopefully, learning from past mistakes, you become a better-upgraded version.

I have reinvented myself quite a few times: I trained and worked in Argentina as an English professor and linguist. I moved to America, where I became an entrepreneur, handbag designer and, later on, a healthcare executive. I moved to the UK, where I continued working in Health and Social Care and moved into international trade. I have been a fashion blogger for some time to support upcoming brands entering the fashion market.

Two years ago, I became a Certified Personal Trainer and pursued a personal ambition not necessarily with a career goal but because I enjoyed it. I became the oldest and most out of shape student, but loved every minute of it. Now I also work as an Indoor Cycling instructor. I seem to enjoy this professional training in a sector that I have no background in. It makes you work harder, allows for non-traditional cross-referencing, and makes you look at opportunities in a different light.

Every time I had to start from scratch; from a point where no one knows you, you have no past, your professional experience does not count, you have no connections, and you realise that only a few people, if any, would be there for you and few others, although willing, cannot really help you.

Life has taught me you are on your own in most situations, and you become the designer of your own destiny. Reinventing myself consisted of understanding myself better and learning what I was good as opposed to what I thought I was good at. Life has taught me that self-awareness is the number one skill and the foundation of any other. Becoming your harshest critic has its rewards, but also significant negatives. You know where to start, and you put together an action plan for yourself; set targets and analyse progress, study challenges, and work on how to overcome them and whether your strategy worked.

My action plans failed many times, and I have to say that hard as it is to accept failure, I have learnt to accept the business side of failure and tried not to take it personally, but this is still a work in progress. I find it difficult to separate myself from who I am as a professional. Some people would call this ambition, and I partially agree with this, but it is also part of your personal development goals and how you plan to grow as an individual. However, I have come across many individuals where this is not even part of who they are, and I admire that about them. However, I could not operate under that premise; I would not know how to do so.

Life is an action plan in which you work 24/7. Action and reaction make your strategy and chisel your persona. This is a non-stop activity and being aware of this is your number one priority.

While building your strategy, you have those around you. Maximising the talent, expertise, and positive energy of those around you has to be key in any master plan. I have been lucky to work and meet highly talented individuals who helped me become a better person and professional. Unfortunately, I have also been close to others who comprised everything I did not want to be. Those you surround yourself with will definitely affect your life. It is everyone's duty to be surrounded by those who only add and whose qualities resonate with you.

I have been more aware of this later in life and more studious about how to meet influential people and connect with them at a professional level and sometimes at a personal level. My strategy for this has been both planned and spontaneous. I have worked on formal business platforms to meet professionals. Still, I have always remembered that no matter who you meet, in whatever setting, there is always a story behind each person; their personal lives, passions and hobbies.

In America, I lobbied in Congress for better healthcare regulations. I met members of Congress and senators, and the conversation flowed from the personal into the business, and in the opposite direction. What has always worked for me is to work hard at getting to know people, not only what they do but also how I can help them. Sometimes it may be just a referral tip or movie recommendation, but it is always a gift of some sort. Paying it forward and giving back is not always about grand gestures but, most of the time, the little ones.

It may sound selfish and self-centred, but in reality, everyone should do this. We should learn from each other and strive to be better, being more generous in sharing our knowledge and passing it on to others.

To conclude: Life has taught me that people make a difference, and I should also make a difference. I should fly against the wind.

My Ten Guiding Principles...

Natasha Preville

I decided to take up the challenge to share the lessons life has taught me; taking a moment of reflection to reveal to all my ten guiding principles that enable me to live, survive, and sometimes, thrive. After all, I want to live the life I love and love the life I live. Yes, there is an element of measured risk in there, but you will come to realise, I walk by faith and not by sight.

As the deadline loomed, amid lockdown, trying to homeschool my children, work on two businesses, be a little more than a ghost of a wife to maintain a modicum of normality, I found myself staring at my laptop...

Okay, Natasha, what lessons has life taught you, lady? I could feel a creeping sense of dread that I may have taken on more than I should have. I already felt overwhelmed with the number of deadlines I had to meet that week, but that is what I do; I overdo it, but I recognise that and it's okay if I am passionate about it.

As the mental download commenced, I could only think of my dear grandmother, currently in the harrowing and relentless grip of dementia. Some days I wonder if it's true; when we see a glimpse of the wonderful, formidable woman we remember that was full of life, wise words, a smile a mile wide and the type of wit that left you gazing in awe (long) after the mic drop...

And with that thought, I am dedicating this piece to my amazing grandmother, Mrs Avis Maud Stephenson, and by the grace of God, she will be here to read this and recognise it as a testament to her influence on my life.

So, I ask: What is a lesson in life? How do we learn? What influences the decisions we make? What calibrates our moral compasses? Is it based solely on our experiences? How do we 'process' achievement and failure? Role models? Self-help books? Positive narratives? For me, it is a constituent of all those parts, and let us not forget, friendly advice, if we are willing to take it.

I was raised to consistently believe I could be anything I wanted to be if I worked hard enough... I consistently believed it too, and for as long as I can remember, I have faced life from that standpoint. I was wholly prepared (and expected) to work harder than my counterparts.

Fine. All I saw around me were hard-working women. They owned everything they had and did, never complained, dressed well, were loved and celebrated, independent, and knew what they wanted in life.

It's notable to add that I have always had an enquiring mind, always looking at all sides, motivation, causes, outcomes, legacies; essentially, a why and wherefores kind of child. I have always been interested in people and the dynamics of human nature/nurture theories, all with a solid allegiance to equality in all its forms. I will highlight the 'lessons' life has taught me by merely listing my most defining ones.

However, I warn you, they are personal, in as far as they are mine… They are what guide my decisions, reactions, actions and thought processes every day, for as long as I can remember… Admittedly, quite a few are from Mrs Stephenson, most certainly the first four, which were linchpins in my early childhood and beyond:

1. Treat Others as You Want to be Treated

This one seems obvious. But if everyone were mindful of it and consciously practised it, the world would be an even greater place to be. On an elementary level, I understood this literally, but as I grew older, I could see the nuances on the reverse. Fundamentally, people would treat you the way you allowed them to treat you. So, I treat everyone I encounter with respect, from the cleaner to the CEO; nothing in it for me, no gains to be had, other than being a decent and respectful human, and more often than not, it is reciprocated.

2. Show Me Your Company and I Will Tell You Who You Are

This was an interesting one… It has kept me on the straight and narrow, even to this day. Be aware of who you let into your inner sanctum – mind, body, and spirit. All is not what it seems… I follow my instincts with close friends and business partners; I want people around me I can trust, those who have shown they have my/our best interests at heart, as I do theirs. Your friends and acquaintances are a reflection of your best self. I keep those close who are not afraid to speak the truth, demonstrating uplifting values, purpose, and visions. People enter my life in seasons for different reasons and that is all fine, but the ones that have stood the test of time are literally a part of me, and I would like to think I am a part of them too, for all the right and authentic reasons.

3. God Bless the Child Who Has His Own

I always wanted to provide for myself, even with a partner. I was independent from an early age and wanted to make my parents and family proud that they were able to raise a self-sufficient human. Even to this day, with a husband I have been with for nearly thirty years, we still have joint and separate bank accounts! I would never change that either. I am not anti-interdependence; however, after the bills, savings and joint reconciliations are sorted, we have license to do as we please with the money/assets we independently have. The very thought of asking for permission or access to funds or the like is alien to me. I am not casting judgement on those that do. Still, the notion of not having a (significant) level of ownership or recourse makes me feel gravely uneasy and gives away my 'power' and personal sustainability.

4. You Can't Be Wrong and Strong

You may have sensed by now that I am no 'wallflower' (ahem)! I am clear in my decisions, thought-processes and opinions, and love sharing them and learning with the willing. However, when you know your position is weak and/or wrong, the strength is in your acceptance of that. All day long, we see people doing wrong and 'showing' strong, regardless. But for me, there is no honour in that; when we are wrong, we are wrong: learn from it and move on.

Interestingly, there is no place this comes to light most in my life than parenting. My husband and I are generally on the same page here, but I have had some 'howler' instances when I have had to back down (at speed). Another book...

5. You <u>Can</u> Have It All (as long as you don't compare yourself to others)

A trickier concept I love to simplify. Yes, you can have it all. <u>You</u> just have to redefine what that is and totally rely on <u>your</u> attributes, ability, and vision. Things become more complicated when you add others to the mix, be it through comparison, companion, or competition. You will *never* win. I have always tried to make myself the best I can be whatever my hopes and aspirations were, the ones I believed I could truly have, only relied on my abilities. Getting married, having children and the like, I hoped for, but always knew there were no guarantees there. However, my happiness, achievements, vision for self, were down to me and only me.

6. Nothing Before Its Time

Perspective and acceptance are biggies. However, the concept occupies more of a cerebral space within me. I am more than aware of my impatient tendencies from time to time, but I am grounded in the fact I know I am where I need to be at any given moment; being mindful of that keeps me level-headed.

One of the most harrowing, debilitating, and painful experiences in my life was when we miscarried twins after we first decided to start a family, following eighteen (happy) years together.

Up to that point in my life, give or take, we had achieved all we wanted to and were now ready to embark on a new journey. Having travelled extensively, completed studies, and established our careers, starting a family did not happen for us as other things had. The feelings of dread, inadequacy, shame, hurt, depression, numbness, and resentment knew no bounds and left an indelible mark on our lives. But I STILL had to believe... That was all I had left... Everything I ever had started with *belief*, and we just held on to that and had faith; if it were meant to be, it will be...

7. What is Meant for You Will Not Pass You By

Noting the previous sentiment, nothing before its time, two and a half years later we were (naturally) blessed with a daughter and then a son, three years after. From then on, I lived by this mantra. I truly believe whatever is meant for you will not pass you by.

Ultimately, life is about choices; arguably, the more you have, the more enriched your life is. But when things have not gone my way, on a particular occasion, as disappointed as I may be in that moment, I believe better is to come. Maybe, given that is my perspective, it has always worked out that way. I try to make sense of most things so I can gain closure, tempting as it is to want to bury your head in the sand, goodness knows, I felt like that most of 2020. I believe things happen for a reason, and there is no such thing as coincidence. The Universe is always teaching me something in the meantime, preparing me to accept my blessings when they (eventually) arrive. Through belief and patience, I will get there.

8. There is No Such Thing as Luck – It's Preparedness Meeting Opportunity

I stopped believing in the concept of luck in my late teens. I distinctly remember overhearing my lecturer practically scold a student for using the term 'luck' concerning another student's exam results. The salient point being my lecturer's retort: "The harder you WORK, the luckier you become." That was all I needed – just work hard, and things will happen.

As the years progressed, reciting my lecturer at every given opportunity in life, I kept working hard and being as prepared as I could be for any fortuitous opportunity that came my way. There was something cathartic and calming about this. It made achievement and success feel real and for the taking, if only you worked hard and stayed prepared, you would be ready to receive. Notwithstanding, putting yourself out there and knowing how to ask for what you want. Another book!

9. FEAR Is Just: False Emotion Appearing Real

Let us not be too literal on this one; yes, you would be right to fear walking into an inferno or jumping off a cliff, or the like. I am talking about when we get in our own way, when our safety nets or comfort zones keep us limited in our beliefs, actions, and teachings; all rooted in fear of the unknown. When we 'know' (or think we do), it comes from a place of reference, be it life experience, advice, upbringing, systemic constructs, etc. When we don't know the outcome and/or something makes us vulnerable, our fears parachute in to protect us and keep us from doing anything different.

However, there is no growth there, just the 'same ole, same ole' to be had. It's only when we shake off the shackles of false emotions appearing real that we genuinely experience growth and awakening.

Take some time to be honest with yourself. Know what fuels your fears in order to overcome them. Regret is my most abhorred emotion, so I go (clean) out of my way to combat my fears, so I don't regret very much at all. Know this, *I am not fearless, I am just not fearful.*

10. *"People will forget what you said, people will forget what you did, but people will never forget how you made them feel."* Maya Angelou

We started with the notion of treating people the way you want to be treated. And to close, I want to focus on how we leave an impression, how we influence and inspire. You only get one chance to make a first impression. Beyond that initial encounter, how are you remembered? It has been said, when people first meet you, either on a personal or professional level, they are only interested in two things; can they trust you? And are you competent? (To do what you say you can, or others have recommended.) I love this because words have power, but instinct, respect, compassion, empathy and perspective are less tangible than words but even more authentic. I want people to not only hear me, but to feel me and my intentions. It's a work in progress, but when I am passionate, when I am alive, I really want you to feel it when I am showing you love (or not).

So here you have it, my ten guiding principles; I wish you every success in finding yours. Be true to yourself and others, be grateful, mark your point of difference, set your intentions in all you do, stand in your power, and share your gifts.

Live the life you love and love the life you live, then enjoy having it all.

Home is Not a Place, it's a Feeling

Minal Srivastava

Growing up in a small, little misty town, I had a very fairy tale notion of life. I believed life was linear, and there was a set process and formula for life and hence success. I was made to believe that if you work hard, study well, ace your exams, be a good girl, then you will end up having a promising career and hence a good life.

I had faith in this promise; I believed in it, and I diligently attacked it like any other task in life, and kept acing one exam after the other. I let myself not get distracted and invested all of myself towards this destination.

That destination for me, which was mentally mapped and planned to a tee and the one that I was visually trying to manifest, ended up with a job and the start of the road to my financial independence and hopeful prosperity. Like in any movie, my story was supposed to have a happy ending. I told myself that story multiple times. I made myself believe in that story.

The sleepy little town had not experienced the wild, worldly success stories, so kids were fed on some distant hope. They were made to push themselves to deliver with the promise of a future which for many in that town had just heard of, and it had become almost like a folklore. Some distant relative, some long-lost friends, who would have left the town in pursuit of a better life and were now the epitome of success. There was not much option in the pre-internet era but to have faith in this promise of a life. There was not a lot to do in that town after school. Colleges were decrepit, the system corrupt, so any child even with a modicum of talent, was pushed to move out and fight the big battle outside. And so, it was for me too.

Eventually, I started my career in Mumbai. A city of dreams for many. A city that apparently never sleeps. I had grown up hearing stories of it. Of the highly improbable, dreamlike success stories and the ruthless, unforgiving failures. A city full of contradictions. Glamour and glitz existing side by side with abject poverty in seemingly complete harmony.

I had not lived in very many cities till then. Neither had I travelled much or seen the world. Mumbai to me was like the window to the world and a life that I was to embark on seemed full of promise. If the story that I had been living off in my head had an ending, then I was reaching the beginning of that phase.

However, very rarely does life pan out the way you visualise it to be as. Age would teach me many lessons later. This would be one of them. But in that moment, I was young, I was naive. In that moment, I had faith, till one day I didn't that is.

I was living alone in the city. I lived with a family as a paying guest, which was essentially a room with a bed, no window, a TV which rarely worked, half a wardrobe, and a fridge shared with the rest of the family. I arrived just after the monsoons had hit the city. It rained consistently, not the unobtrusive, gentle, cold rains that I was used to and had experienced in the small little town on a hill that I grew up in. The rains in Mumbai were an attention seeker. À propos to the city vibes, even the rains came in with a lot of drama, unbridled pomp, and fury. In my dark, dank room, I could hear it beating down on the roof, the road and pavement throughout the night.

I worked like a dog which is what a fresher is apparently supposed to do, and I followed the rule book yet again. Bone tired, late into the night, I would board the local train for Andheri and then walk along Four Bungalows' leafy lanes to the lonely, dark, small, dank room of mine. I was surprised by the independence and safety that the city offered to a young girl; those walks late into the night, all alone, felt empowering. Sometimes, you do not even realise what you are missing till it is handed to you. Walking safely on the roads without the fear of a predator lurking behind you was one such freedom that I had not experienced or acknowledged to myself that I was missing on.

I was in the most happening city in the country with an amazing nightlife. I was in a city which allowed me and any young girl to walk alone in its lanes, late into the night. It was kind to strugglers and outsiders, mostly – it let them be. For many, even that was a relief. I also had all the freedom which I didn't know what to do with. For the first time in my life, I was financially independent, but there was this persistent, nagging feeling which I could not manage to shake off.

Despite the body being tired, I did not manage to let my mind calm down in those months. Long, sleepless nights, I would lie down and listen to the angry tirade of the monsoon storm outside. Frequently, the water would seep through the gap just underneath the wooden door. I would place a thick towel to help stop the flow.

Somehow, all my life, I had been preparing for this moment and this phase. It felt very anti-climactic. All of it was very confusing. All my life, I had not allowed myself to look beyond this destination. I felt I had been cheated by life.

As a fresher starting off from the bottom of any corporate ladder, you are taught and trained not to question.

Your job is to follow instructions, almost blindly. You have no visibility on how that is adding any value to the business, your life, or the world in general. That leads to dissonance. With no particular fault of the system here, since that is how most organisations are built, there is a lot of focus on structures, formats, and processes, and not enough bandwidth or patience to train a newcomer and hone their individuality.

Instead, the attempt is to conform, fix and set everyone in few confined boundaries of roles and behaviours. That is how an organisation achieves scale. Very soon an organisation starts running like a piece of well-oiled machinery, and individuality does not usually play a very significant role. Especially when you are young and are yet not too sure on who you are and what you want from life, the initial few months in any job can be quite confusing. And so it was for me too.

More than the work which was a lot because as a fresher, you are right at the bottom of the "food chain" and hence end up doing all the grudge work, the utter uselessness of it tired me. Or that's how I viewed it then. I had no other visibility. I did not know if my work was contributing towards anything.

However, the most vivid memory for me of that phase is the ride on the local train at night. With my head pressed against the window, I would voyeuristically peer outside in the dark into the houses we passed by, with everyday life going on, with full-fledged families in it. Kids in front of television, mothers chopping vegetables in the kitchen, families having dinner. Those slices of lives illuminated under yellowish bulbs had me deeply yearning for something so badly, which in those moments, I couldn't put a finger on.

I had a job that I felt was meaningless and I had no friends or family around me. However, the most disheartening of all, which I realised much later in life, was that I had lost my purpose. Up till that moment, I was running towards a defined destination, and suddenly that imagery was not in sync with what I always had faith on and was made to believe.

Later, life would teach me that this is what will matter the most. Not the destination. Not rewards but if you just believe in what you are running towards. It will take me years to differentiate between making a living and living a life. I will pin my identity to a job, a designation, and I will live that lie. I will once again tell myself a story and make myself believe that story so that I will be glued to the race with all my heart and soul, year after year. In the process, I will lose myself. And the chance at any meaningful relationship.

Then, just like that, one day, I will become a mother. A reluctant one to begin with. An unprepared and a scared one. I will stumble through it. I will resent it at times. I will sink to the lowest low while I have a deep battle within, all the while trying to unravel what should be an ideal definition of life and career. I will struggle to balance the two. I will want to ace the two roles. I will treat motherhood like any other exam in life.

However, slowly and gradually, that tiny little life will chip at all my rough edges. Technically, I will be the parent, but I will be the one being taught and trained in the process. Every single notion and format of what I had been told about life will change. I will learn. I will grow. I will change and I will accept it.

And then, one day, I will fall in love with this new version of myself and life.

Much later, I will remember those lonely rides on the local trains, voyeuristically peeking into slices of lives through fleeting window frames. Much later, I will accept to myself that I was not searching for money, fame, or power, but was pining for a family and love in that moment. It will take me years to realise that the almost primitive, deep yearning was not so much for constructing a house, but the concept of a home.

It will take me very many years to not feel cheated by life anymore. I will look back at all those years very frequently. I will think of the lonely, disillusioned young girl staring out of the train window at the slices of family life illuminated under yellow bulbs and I will want to hug and reassure her that, one day, she will be home.

Yes, I am home!

You Would Be Prettier if You Were White

Natalie Heilling

My name is Natalie Heilling. I am a mother, a business owner, and a survivor who turned an emotionally difficult early childhood into a mindset of perseverance.

Without realising it, I had gone into adult life, having successfully buried the trauma of my early childhood, in which both my family and I were extremely racially abused.

It was only because of recent events, with the Black Lives Matter movement, where I could see emotions running high across the world, that I had the courage to revisit these dark times. As I watched protests sweep across nations, it became apparent that people demanded to have their voices heard and wanted to speak out against racism. What I found moving was the unity – people from all different nationalities and walks of life coming together to voice that they did not find this type of behaviour acceptable.

It was the magnifying glass I needed to look at my own background and examine it deeply. It was like a light bulb moment, and for once, I looked at my young self and smiled. I had finally found the courage to observe my past critically, accept it, both the good and the bad, and not be ashamed of who I was growing up.

I grew up in Hertfordshire, one of three children of bi-racial parents. My father is British, and my mum is from Trinidad. In the 1960s, our parents were married in Britain. When I think back to my childhood, rather than remembering playing outside in a carefree manner with my friends, I remember always being on guard from who might appear around the corner, a feeling of anxiety over what might happen to me.

What I clearly remember from my childhood is that we were the only family of colour in our community. We grew up on a council estate. Although decent people were living there, we experienced extreme incidents of racism involving groups of people following and tormenting us, emotional and verbal abuse, and horrific violent acts against my pets and my mother.

I remember one particular incident that happened when I was five years old. One afternoon, I was playing in the park at the back of our house with my brother and some friends. Suddenly our neighbours' teenage sons and a group of their friends came out of nowhere and surrounded us. This was also a pretty common occurrence, in that anytime we were out on the estate playing, the news would spread of our location so that groups of people would turn up and target us with verbal abuse and threats of violence. This occasion was no different. It started with verbal abuse, but before I knew it, a teenage boy kicked me in the face with full force. His foot landed right under my eye, and the pain and shock were unbearable. This has left me with a permanent scar under my eye.

There were also times when our neighbours had come into our back garden and put glass in my paddling pool, which I almost went into until my older sibling realised just in time. On the same day, I had also found my pet turtle with his shell smashed to pieces.

These incidents were genuinely shocking and something that no one should ever have to experience.

I was often made to feel ashamed of how I looked, who I was, and where I came from throughout my childhood. I was also the only child of colour in primary school, and I remember frequently being told by my friends that "you would be prettier if you were white".

These experiences haunted me for many years. Events like this naturally make it difficult for you to feel accepted in any setting. On top of this, you question yourself and what people think about you all the time. It resulted in me having a lack of self-belief, low self-esteem, and acute anxiety in many settings.

As we no longer felt safe in our own home, eventually, we moved to a different neighbourhood. Although my confidence was utterly shattered, things started to get better after that. Although I still felt an undercurrent of racism from time to time, as we were still the only family of colour, it was in a much lower key. In general, the community was very accepting.

Luckily, later in life, I met wonderful friends and work colleagues who, without even knowing it, rebuilt my confidence, self-esteem and faith in people. This, coupled with the recent events linked to George Floyd, Breonna Taylor, Ahmaud Arbery, and all others who had to experience senseless acts of injustice, has made me realise that I no longer can be ashamed of who I am, where my parents come from, or the colour of my skin.

Unfortunately, there is a world of people who will continue to suffer this injustice. Still, hopefully, with the growing number of voices across the world ready to take a stand against this type of behaviour, things will continue to improve.

Today, I feel different. Today, I am thankful for who I am. I am glad to be different and proud of all that I have achieved. Strangely, I feel that the negative experiences taught me resilience. If I were to think of areas in which life has taught me most, it would be below:

1. Channel negative experiences into a positive mindset.

Throughout my student years and adult working life, I have tried my best to harness this negative experience into a positive and tenacious mindset of never giving up. It is not all about that, though; we also must find it in ourselves to forgive people's behaviour, even if they did us wrong. This can apply to many settings, from racism to all aspects of toxic relationships and abuse. As the saying goes, to hold on to hate is like drinking poison. It is crucial to pick yourself up and move forward. What does not break you will strengthen you, and the more you see positive results in your everyday life, harness this to help drive you on even further.

2. Become aware of your thoughts and any limiting beliefs and work to remove them.

I feel that any situation involving abuse, points to the importance of working on yourself in whichever way you need to remove any painful blockers or memories that will prevent you from moving forward. I found a lot of my answers in meditation. This may sound a bit too spiritual for some people, but it is vital to love yourself and not constantly beat yourself up or have self-doubt. When we live by negative emotions created by some past event, this drives our behaviours to become negative, and as a reflection of that, our behaviours will be self-limiting. It is essential to remove those blockers and realise that they do not define you. With a plan, the right behaviours, and action, we can have the life or career we want. It just all starts with a mindset, commitment, and action. You can create any destiny that you want.

3. You cannot change people. Only they can change themselves.

It is difficult when someone has suffered any kind of abuse. I was a people-pleaser for many years, and I am also a complete empath. However, life has taught me that no matter what we do as individuals, we can never please everyone, and we should not beat ourselves up about it when that is the case. It has also taught me that no matter how nice or humble we might be, there will still be people out there that will not like you for any reason. I make sure not to let other people's negativity affect me and focus on positives, on how I want to treat people, and what I want to achieve in my own life.

I can't change what happened to me, but I feel we have a choice after going through such traumatic events, to either let those experiences define who we become, or we can choose to rise above them. For me, I chose the latter. I did not want to become defined by my past. I also did not want my children to follow their life path with that mentality. I feel it is important to lead by example in any area of your life, whether that be in the workplace or within your own family.

Today, I am thankful for having two wonderful daughters. We live in London, and the population is much more diverse, meaning that, luckily, they have not had to endure such treatment. However, I always make sure to teach them they should be proud of their heritage and who they are.

As you can imagine, I am hot on the topic of diversity. Having this experience has also helped me find my purpose in running a business that I LOVE. I am conscious of the broad array of issues that have to be considered when companies put together their Diversity and Inclusion strategies. I co-founded Research Partners, an Executive Search and Talent Intelligence company. We are encouraged to see that the corporate world recognises the benefits of having a diverse gender and cultural workforce.

My experience has fostered my genuine desire of helping clients with solutions that will ensure companies excel in this area, whilst making it a positive experience for the candidates.

I am proud of our team at Research Partners, as we have created an incredibly diverse culture of like-minded people who show mutual respect for our clients, candidates, and colleagues alike.

Over recent years, I also focus my time outside of work to help others break free from trauma and limiting beliefs that are holding them back from living their full potential. I am a Certified Quantum Flow Practitioner. I am passionate about spiritual healing and have a keen interest in neuroscience, mindset work and personal development.

Life does not always go as planned, but the beauty of this is that it can surprise you with beautiful and positive events at any moment. The key is to keep moving forward, knowing that you can control your destiny with positive emotions and behaviours. That life will get better – as long as we work hard, treat people how we expect to be treated, and experience the feeling of being alive.

Here's to everyone dedicated to fighting for a kinder world in which to live.

Perfection is the Enemy

Geri Maroney

They say that life is a journey and not a destination. I remember early in my career thinking that this quote was wrong. For me, each of my career goals was a destination that I would celebrate and check off my list before moving onto the next goal. I never stayed long at these individual destinations, but I recognised and celebrated each one of them. The challenge was to keep moving, to keep going from one destination to the next.

From early on, I always knew what I wanted from my life; I wanted a successful career and the perfect family. It seemed simple. That's how it works, right? You grow up, work hard, become successful, and live happily ever after. Well, not exactly.

Although I can honestly say that I have accomplished my goals of having a successful career, a happy family, and a great life, I must admit at specific points along the way that I nearly abandoned my goals because the burden was too heavy. Things were not easy, and at certain points, my life became very turbulent. I think this is true for nearly everyone; we have a plan for life, and then life has a plan for us.

As I reminisce on my career, I am thankful for the opportunities that I had and for the challenges presented to me along the way. I had the good fortune of learning from some great mentors who challenged me to step outside my comfort zone and grow into a better, stronger person. Now I realise I may not have been able to conquer my fears and achieve the level of success that I did without them.

Fear is a compelling emotion. The fear of being judged. The fear of saying something stupid or being laughed at by others. The fear of not being perfect. Fear stops people from moving forward, sometimes for just a little while and sometimes for their entire lives.

I learned that an important way to ease fear was to give up the notion of being perfect. Achieving perfection is, after all, just an illusion. I am thankful that I learned this early in my career. However, there is a difference between always striving for the top score on the annual employee evaluation and being "perfect". They are not the same thing. One should always do one's best and strive for high scores, but don't spend too much time trying to achieve perfection.

I remember working hard on a significant, high-profile project that I was nervous about because my audience was executive-level leaders. The project was the first of its kind for this company. I remember my boss telling me, "Don't wait until your idea is 100% perfect. Get it 80% of the way there and then implement it. You'll figure out the other 20% along the way. You know more about this subject than anyone else in the room, so trust yourself. Do the work, analyse the situation, make a recommendation and then go for it."

That advice helped me a lot, and I still lean on those words today. Trying to achieve perfection requires too much extra time and energy. When you are hyper-focused on the minor details, the project (or decision) becomes too big and too draining, and it can prevent you from moving forward. Perfectionism also leads to black or white thinking, with no middle ground. It is either perfect, or it isn't. This mentality is unproductive. Instead, try to focus on the progress you have made and trust yourself to make the right decision. Get it 80% of the way there, and then just move forward.

So, I completed the project, made the presentation to the senior leaders, and received excellent feedback. Some said that I explained the complex problem in a way that they had never heard before and that it was easy to follow and made wonderful sense. They complimented me on my authentic style, and we walked away with the approval we needed to move forward!

I took a big chance, and through the process, I learned to trust myself. I learned to be authentic and to have a well thought-out opinion that I could defend. My mentor would always tell me I didn't necessarily have to be right in my opinion, but I had to have an opinion, be willing to express it, and be willing to defend it to those who might disagree. These words helped me be thorough in my approach and make sure I had thought of both sides of the argument before moving forward. I learned to listen to others speak instead of immediately forming my response. I learned to discuss issues and come to a consensus with healthy, thoughtful debate.

In July 2015, I was diagnosed with breast cancer, and my cancer journey strengthened many of the important lessons I had already learned about giving up perfectionism and trusting myself. Still, it also taught me new lessons about courage, trust and forgiveness. Cancer taught me the real meaning of strength. Think about what scares you the most in your life and then step into that space. That's what cancer feels like emotionally. Through my journey, I learned to let go of anger and forgive both myself and others. Cancer gave me a profound appreciation for what it meant to be strong and a clear lens of what was most important in my life.

Going back to the notion of perfectionism, you must let it go. People most often do their best with what they know. If someone hurt you, or a situation didn't turn out the way you wanted it to, I encourage you to forgive. Forgive yourself, forgive others, and try to heal so that you can move forward in a healthy way. Anger can destroy you, and carrying the past only makes for a hefty load and an unhealthy spirit.

Stretch beyond your comfort zone. Always be open to learning new things. Go to the border of where you are comfortable and then step past it. It will feel scary at first, but I promise, if you do it once, you will learn to do it again and again. This approach is how you grow, both professionally and personally.

If you want the new promotion, then tell your boss. Ask them for their help in mentoring you so that they can prepare you for the next promotion. Be your own biggest cheerleader. Think forward and be innovative. If you want to achieve a specific goal, think about a few different strategies that might get you there. I always encourage people to have a Plan A and a Plan B. From experience, Plan A usually gets modified anyway, so be flexible and have a good backup strategy for achieving your goal. Flexibility is essential and learning that early in your career gives you an added advantage. Be ready to pivot.

Be your own best friend. When I was diagnosed with cancer, I did not clearly understand the emotional challenges that came along with a breast cancer diagnosis. Of course, I understood the physical challenges, but I highly underestimated the emotional challenges I would face. Many people think that once you are done with your cancer surgery, it should be over. They think you don't have cancer anymore and that you should just move forward. But that is not actually how the cancer journey goes. A cancer diagnosis is much more of a one-step-forward/two-steps-back kind of journey.

Through my journey, I had to rediscover who I was and what I wanted out of my life. PTSD is a common side effect of hearing the words "you have cancer," and it hit me extremely hard. I was grateful that my doctor had warned me about it, so when it happened, I knew what it was. I was starting over with my cancer survivor life, and I learned more about the strength of self-determination than I had learned in all my years before cancer. I learned the importance of leaning on others for strength and courage, and I learned I wasn't responsible for solving all the world's problems!

Of course, I knew all the problems were not mine to solve, but I sure tried hard to help! During my healing, I learned to focus first on myself before others. We hear this repeatedly, but I can tell you from personal experience, it is true. We must first focus on ourselves and then on helping others. The saying "You can't pour from an empty cup" is accurate, and through cancer, I learned to have an open heart and make myself strong before moving forward to help others. It's just liked the flight attendant says, "Put your mask on first, before helping others." There is absolute truth to this.

Knowing what lights you up and what feeds your soul is a crucial step to getting unstuck and finding the energy and excitement to launch yourself forward towards greater satisfaction and success in your life, both personally and professionally. If you hate what you are doing, then stop doing it. If you dream of being something else, then be it. We have a limited amount of time to make our dreams come true, and cancer taught me not to waste that precious gift. Do what makes your heart sing.

Find your tribe. Hang out with people you love. Who we choose to spend time with is one of the most important decisions in our lives. There is an old saying by Vladimir Lenin that says, "Show me your friends, and I'll tell you who you are." This is so true and should be taken seriously.

We lean on our friends a lot; we share our successes, challenges, and defeats with them. They are a primary source of support and encouragement for us. Make sure they are the right people. If you are hanging out with the Debbie-downer, you might have difficulty finding the bright side. Surround yourself with people who will help you reach your goals. This includes personal and professional goals. Business networking is critical to business success in the same way that having a robust personal support system is vital to your personal life. Find your people, and soon you will see that you gain strength and confidence from them.

Please pay it forward. I have always been an excellent teacher, and I enjoy mentoring others. I am of the notion that what you give comes back to you, so I continue to mentor young professionals and advocate for breast cancer awareness. We are stronger together, and I always encourage people to share their gifts with others. Read books to children, teach teenagers, mentor young professionals, or spend time with the elderly. Whatever it is, find something you are good at and offer your services to better our communities. Be positive and be helpful. Leave the world a better place.

Life – Your World or Your Prison?

Christopher Weguelin

"Without risk, nothing new ever happens.
Without trust, fear creeps in.
Without serendipity, there are no surprises."
Rita Gelman –
American author

Introduction

"Life's lessons" are extreme; they can bring happiness or heartbreak, success or failure. They are lessons learned that deal with an individual's emotional intelligence (EQ) rather than intellectual knowledge or material possessions.

In today's world, what we perceive to be our rights has become intertwined with the basic and core principles of what a naked human can achieve. There are two types of lessons we categorise as "Life's lessons," and these are:

a. Those that we have created, such as the need for ever more wealth, possessions, material assets, titles, and social standing
b. Those that have existed since the beginning of humanity, driven by our fears of hunger, sickness, loneliness, and our basic needs to live (or emotional intelligence)

Background

I have always considered myself fortunate to have had a privileged childhood, not such a successful education and a professional life that allowed me to experience different environments. I was fortunate to meet and work with some inspiring and very talented people. It was at times challenging and pushed me to the boundaries of my abilities; however, it was rewarding and enjoyable.

I could use the same summary for my private life: some memorable moments of fun, friendship, laughter, becoming a husband (twice), becoming a father of four children with corresponding moments of despair, anger, divorce (twice), loneliness, and lack of confidence, to name a few.

My professional career began when I was seventeen, after the rather unspectacular end to a standard education with a temporary position as a farm labourer on a local farm. Following a chance meeting after one month, I enrolled on a one-day-a-week course, "Farming for Beginners," suitably impressing my employer enough to make my contract permanent. Over the next five years, with a mix of work experience and attending full-time college, I achieved a diploma in Farm and Business Management. I held the Assistant Manager position on one of the largest private-owned estates in central Southern England, but after five years on the estate, curiosity got the better of me. I enrolled myself on a computer programming evening course and subsequently managed from specification to installing a computer system in the estate office.

After assessing the long-term future of farming, I was granted a position on a three-month intensive business programming course and ended my career in agriculture. Over the next ten to twelve years, I worked for three accounting software providers in a range of different roles from programming, customer support, project management, services manager, and operations director overseeing projects such as service configurations, ISO accreditations, supplier accreditation, selection setup, and implementation of management team. I was fortunate to have the opportunities I did and could take the ones I felt were the best fit for me when there were others I declined. By the end of 2001, things were looking good.

The Beginning of an Adventure

As the annual haze of post-new year celebrations cleared in January 2002, a case could easily have been made which would have been hard to argue against, that I enjoyed some of the more materialistic benefits of life.

To this day, I do not know why, but sometime during that February, I started waking in the mornings with a feeling that something was missing. My current job was challenging and exciting, the salary was excellent, I knew one owner of the company, I had a great private life in terms of friendships and socialising activities, and I was fit and my cupboards were full.

Over the next two months, what formed in my mind was a genuine desire to travel. At first, I tried to ignore it, but I still woke with the same feeling every morning. Finally, I approached the owner, and after a pretty lengthy discussion, he said he would speak to his business partner and come back to me within a week. In my mind, I was secretly hoping he would provide the solution to my dilemma by asking me to postpone the trip, in which case I would look disappointed but agree, and the topic would disappear.

One week later, we had another discussion in which he outlined a backup plan agreed upon with his partner. They identified people they wanted me to split my workload with and, with a big smile, informed me I worked too many hours for too long. I deserved the break; enjoy it! One part of me wanted to jump up and down and dance with happiness, whilst the other half was asking, "What the hell have you just done?!"

Over the next six months, I fulfilled my handover obligations at work, informed my family and friends, who were all incredibly supportive (except for my father, who could not comprehend such action – this was to be expected), put my house on the market to rent and slowly packed everything away. I went shopping every weekend, brought my plane ticket, and decided I would only commit to one definite objective, which was to visit Sydney, Australia. Albeit at the last minute, but much to the pleasure of the nurse who relished the opportunity to stick multiple needles into another human being, I got the relevant preventions for travelling throughout Asia and Australia.

I decided my first stop would be Bangkok, as Thailand had been open to mass tourism from Europe for a long time. I deemed it to be a safe starting point until about three weeks before departure when a UK tourist was mugged at a beach resort I was planning to visit. With all the support and encouragement I was getting, my confidence was soaring, and I was not changing my plans.

Two weeks before I was due to leave, a friend approached me as she had arranged a two-week holiday in Thailand arriving the day after me; however, her friend had to cancel at the last minute, and she asked if I could wait for her arrival, and I could spend these weeks with her. This made wonderful sense to me as well, and so I finished work on a Friday. After two long nights of goodbyes and a lot of beer, I flew off on a once-in-a-lifetime journey, now feeling a sense of freedom and being some kind of adventurer heading into uncharted waters; it was such an exciting feeling.

The day after I arrived in Bangkok, I met up with my friend, and after a day to adapt and recover from the flight, we headed north to Chiang Mai, where we visited some temples, went on day trips and witnessed the annual Loy Krathong festival of lights, sharing the evenings with other holidaymakers we met during the days. Shortly after the festival, people left and then finally I got up early one morning, took my friend to the airport and said goodbye to the last person from the life I was leaving behind for the next twelve months. After taking a shower at the hostel and going out to the market to eat some food from the street vendors, I spent the rest of the day chilling out sorting my bags before going out on my first real night alone on an adventure that had started as some annoying dream when I woke up to one morning eight months earlier, that I did not understand but would not go away.

I woke the following day with two feelings: first, I had not slept well, which was not surprising because it was about 4:00 am and I had only slept for three hours, and second, not knowing where I was. I put both down to excitement and nerves. Still, I was restless the whole day. When the same thing happened the next night, I started to question what was going on, and after the third night when I woke again, I was feeling frightened, and I questioned myself, "What am I doing? Where am I going?" and then the big one, "How do I travel?"

The more I thought about what was happening, the more I was being overwhelmed with fear. I started to think about home, but I could not go back. My house was rented, and I had been very clear with the family that I would be gone for between ten to twelve months. I had resigned my position at work; there was nothing to go back to – who could I call after three days on my own? The answer was… no one. How would that look? Panic was setting in. I just wanted to go to the airport and fly home, but I would not let myself do that.

For the next ten days, I got up early every day to avoid people, left the hostel on foot and walked for hours through streets and in the surrounding countryside, sometimes with tears just running down my cheeks; the local tuk-tuk drivers called me the "Crazy Englishman" as I walked past them every morning. "All you do is walk, walk and walk in the sun and the heat," one told me. "We see you everywhere walking."

Slowly I calmed down and whilst trying to work out what was happening, I wrote down four questions I needed to answer: What had I done? Why had I done it? Why was I feeling like this? What was I going to do about it?

1. What had I done?

The answer to this first question was, I had just abandoned everything I had worked for since the first day I started working on a farm. My parents had brought me up with a strong work ethic which included being committed, loyal, hard-working, respecting your employers, being on time and not taking days off with false excuses. I had abandoned my children, though they were the ones who took me to the airport and waved goodbye to me, happy that I was doing something for myself, and I left behind friends and a personal life that had developed over the years.

2. Why had I done it?

I had done it because, for the twenty-eight years since I started working, I had never taken my full quota of annual holiday. I never took time for myself apart from odd days or a week here or there. I had worked weekends and bank holidays, and I always wanted to be there if the children needed something. Now, I wanted to do something for myself, but suddenly it sounded very selfish.

3. Why was I feeling like this?

Initially, this was the hardest question to answer until slowly I realised I was not missing my Mercedes company car, I was not missing going to work, I was not missing my wardrobe full of clothes (which, on my return home, I put in one pile that nearly covered the entire floor of my spare room, some items I had only worn once, a lot I did not even recognise and would never have brought them again), or my gadgets. I could call my family and friends whenever I wanted, and then I realised I was missing something I had never considered before which was… emotional intelligence.

The basic principles of a human being are to fend for themselves, and I was a forty-five-year-old human with a child's emotional capability outside of the bubble I had been living in, where so much is done automatically and so much can be hidden behind bravado and material items, but so much for practical purposes is also worthless. I had often said for challenges at work or sometimes at home, "That took me outside of my comfort zone," which was an overstatement. Being outside of my comfort zone was where I found myself in those days in Chiang Mai, having to think, decide and take actions for myself with no guidelines, no template, and no point of reference. "It was me versus me."

4. What was I going to do about it?
Having answered questions 1–3, the one thing I would not do was give up and go home. I was not going back until I had achieved the one goal I had set for myself, which was to reach Sydney. Once I had this back in focus, things fell into place. I realised this was a bigger opportunity to develop myself than I had ever imagined. I had to take this opportunity to run around and take pictures, and learn and develop new skills. I also realised I could not do this on my own; I would need to research things, ask questions, trust people who would probably ask me questions, and be prepared to help whenever

possible. I now knew that I wanted to return home from this once-in-a-lifetime opportunity to share experiences and learn fundamental lessons from other people that I could apply to everyday life. I also promised myself I would enjoy it.

Two days later, I boarded the train from Chiang Mai to Bangkok, which was the real beginning of the journey that started as a dream and had already taught me the biggest life lesson that I had faced on my own. I completed my trip, and was on the way to achieving the one goal I had set myself. I had so many experiences, some alone but many shared with others. As I stood on top of the Sydney Harbour Bridge, I thought of the three fundamentals that had got me there and to where I am today.

1. **Risk** – everyone has to take risks in daily life, but many risks are determined for us, and much of our upbringing trains us how to overcome them. However, to experience new things, one has to assess the risks, make a judgement, and accept the responsibility.
2. **Trust** – is generally spoken in reference to two parties trusting each other. What I learnt was that before that trust can be built between two parties, every individual must trust themselves. From trust comes respect, and the foundation for any relationship, either professional or personal. Broken trust in others can be rebuilt. Trust in oneself is harder because one has to accept the

responsibility and recognise that changes are necessary. Unlike trusting others, you can never walk away from yourself.

As someone once told me, *"Your last decision was not the wrong decision, you might have to make another decision, but the last decision will always be better than no decision."*

3. **Serendipity** – in business, the preferred term is opportunism, which is often thought of as a lucky chance. In business, you have a goal and to reach that, related opportunities can arise. Serendipity, on the other hand, is coming across and recognising opportunities not foreseen or expected and not related, that can offer benefits. Serendipity can much more easily pass by unnoticed, and more often requires bigger changes to earn the benefits.

To summarise… Keep an open mind, and look out for serendipity with a willingness to change direction, whilst assessing the risk and trusting your judgement and decision-making.

What happened after?

Eleven months after I departed, I returned to the UK, moved back into my house and started up a business offering business and IT consultancy. A year later, an ex-colleague asked if I would assist with a small part of a migration project based in Zurich for five to six weeks. This was sixteen years ago, and my last position with the same company was as Finance Director, responsible for four European markets.

Was there any evidence that I had actually learnt anything from that Journey?

Two moments stand out as they immediately made me reflect on that year's travelling. First, after about four years in Switzerland, a local colleague left the company and at his leaving party, he came to me and said he would like to thank me for a couple of things; I didn't have a clue as to what he was going to say.

He said, "Firstly, I would like to thank you for teaching us to enjoy coming to work; even in the toughest meetings, you managed to break the ice with a comment and a smile without offending or being disrespectful. Secondly, for demonstrating that when mistakes are made, being honest enough to accept your responsibility whilst offering a solution is better than trying to hide the problem or blame someone else."

Laughing in the workplace had been frowned upon, and admitting a mistake was considered a weakness. I still hold these as part of my most rewarding achievements because they were not achieved by reaching figures or deadlines, but by managing my emotional intelligence. I had no previous experience or knowledge of Emotional Intelligence, but it was something I became aware of and developed during those months alone in various situations in different countries and various cultures.

To Be Strong Does Not Mean to Be Insensitive

Gabrielle Botelho

T he big challenge is how to take care of our emotions so that they are catalysts of our potential, rather than inhibitors of our growth.

I was born in a small town in the countryside near Rio de Janeiro, Brazil. I grew up in a very structured home, with strong examples of ethical and moral conduct.

My father, a skilled worker, could not complete his studies. He lost his family at an early age. After his mother died, he was separated from his father at the age of seven. His father, who was in poor health, financially could not raise his children, so my father and his six brothers were raised by different families of distant cousins or uncles and started interacting only in adult life.

Mr Botelho, as my father was known, was always a fortress. He was a very strict person, and I do not remember seeing him cry even once. Later, I understood that the lack of tears did not mean a lack of feelings, because every person feels differently. He always said, "When I get older, I will go to a retirement home because I don't want to be a burden on anyone's life." Ironically, he died of brain cancer, which compromised his basic functions, and he had to be taken care of by nurses and his family until the last day of his life.

My mother was a person of impressive sweetness, care, and affection. Tirelessly, she always lived for the family, giving up her own needs, and putting her husband's and children's wishes first. She was a teacher, but her big dream had been to become a lawyer. She did not pursue her goal because she did not want my father to feel inferior. Do you know that old saying, "Behind a great man, there is always a greater woman"? Well, my mother was that great woman. She always lived in the shadow of my father, but by working, she achieved her financial independence and could continue to give to her children the things she could not give herself.

Known as D. Terezinha (or Grandma Terê, as her grandchildren affectionately called her), my mother has always been my most significant sponsor, supporter, and safe haven. She helped me embark on all my dreams and helped me conquer them all. I was lucky to have the example of such a strong and sweet woman. When I was still a child back in the eighties, I remember her telling me, "My daughter, your first husband has to be your job, your profession. Marry and be committed to yourself first."

At twenty-one, I left my hometown to go to Rio de Janeiro to study Psychology at the Federal University of Rio de Janeiro. This was like a dream come true; a dream of being independent, building my own story, and not just being seen as an heir to my parents. I adopted Rio de Janeiro as my own city, where I studied, grew as a professional, made many friends, got married, and got divorced. However, this marriage, which some may consider as being unsuccessful, I still found very successful. It gave me two beautiful children, Miguel and Maria Clara, who are the reason for everything.

My life in Rio had always been challenging. Living alone and being away from home was my choice, but I paid a high price for it. I missed many memorable moments, birthdays, and times that I will never get back. I remember weekends were difficult. I hated Sundays because of that, and I missed being with my family. Similarly, life in the countryside greatly differed from living in the "big city".

I learned a lot through trial and error. I was very insecure, naive, and afraid of everything. However, I began making my own decisions little by little; right or wrong, they were mine, and I was proud of my trajectory. Among many missteps and teachings, I became the person I am today. There are innumerable teachings and lessons that I have learned throughout my life, and I am sure that I will continue learning until the end.

However, here I would like to highlight the importance of being attentive and taking care of our emotions along the way. Emotional intelligence has a fundamental role and can make a real difference in our lives. Therefore, I went back to my origins to understand my history and better identify my triggers and behaviours.

Being raised by strong and rigid parents with such high standards made me strong on the outside and fragile on the inside. That feeling of "I'm not good enough" or "I need to try harder" and "I'm not ready yet" followed me for a long time. Self-validation, self-acceptance, and self-love were all conditional to me – conditional on continuous performance and maximum delivery, on the personal and professional side.

On a personal level, I remember precisely when I felt this need for self-validation for the first time. I was still studying, and I had to move to my second apartment in Rio. I had just six hours to complete the entire move; otherwise, it would cost me additional money. I was alone, without knowing many people in the city, but I had to do it. I worked extremely hard that day, but I completed the move in time. It was after this episode that I heard, for the first time, my father saying that he was very proud of me.

Therefore, I believed I would be loved if I could accomplish great things, that my parents would be proud of and love me for that, rather than unconditionally. Later, studying Positive Intelligence, I understood that this belief was one of my biggest saboteurs.

Author and executive coach Shirzad Chamine created Positive Intelligence (PQ) based on recent ideas and discoveries from neuroscience, psychology, cognitive behavioural psychology, and the area of high-performance study. The PQ shows the ability to control our mind and how well it works in our own interests.

According to Chamine, the mind operates in two ways: one positive (wise) and the other negative (saboteur). The "wise man" sees challenges as opportunities, producing curiosity, empathy, and calm. "Saboteurs" cause stress, anxiety, and insecurity. These are mechanisms to help us survive the real and imagined threats during the first phase of our life.

Therefore, as adults, we no longer need them, but the patterns of thinking, feeling, and the reaction of our "saboteurs" become encoded in our brains. The first step to ending this cycle of "dependency" is to identify which "saboteur" has manifested itself more frequently in your life. It is about bringing to light what hides in the shadow.

For a long time, we have been discussing the importance of our emotions in our life. In line with Daniel Goleman's theory, Emotional Intelligence is the ability to manage our relationships and ourselves effectively. It comprises four fundamental capabilities: self-awareness, self-management, social awareness, and social skill.

For Goleman, the entire process of developing EI starts with self-knowledge, which he defines as emotional self-knowledge, accurate self-assessment, and self-confidence.

In my case, this characteristic of being a person who makes it happen, focusing strongly on delivery and results, has accompanied me since the beginning of my professional career. I was seen as a person able to deliver "no matter what," and I liked to have this professional image.

However, that competence ended up becoming a label, and instead of boosting my career, it was a professional growth inhibitor. Concluding, my greatest strength was preventing me from reaching my full potential. In this sense, I realised that I must improve my self-knowledge, self-criticism, and confidence, to keep growing and developing professionally.

In the last five years, I have immersed myself in the process of self-knowledge. It happened first from the inside when I realised I should get to know myself better. I started questioning who I was, and what kind of legacy I would like to leave my kids. By this time, I worked for a great company in an excellent position, but I was not happy. I knew that I should change and add some missing pieces to my life, but I did not know how to change them.

I started reading many books that could give me a broader view of beliefs, spirituality, life philosophy, and give me an idea about brain functioning. I also started some meditation practices that helped me recognise my emotions better and reflect on my current choices.

However, this self-knowledge process would not be complete without a perception from the outside because how I see myself can differ from others' views. Therefore, I asked for support from my friends and family, people I trusted that could give honest feedback. They shared their perceptions about my behaviours and impulses, helping me perform a complete evaluation, considering both internal and external parameters.

This feedback process was hard for me. To face what people genuinely think about you can sometimes hurt. In my case, I had to practice active listening. Hearing is involuntary, but listening is a choice. I listened to my beloved ones' feedback to learn from their perspectives and not reply or defend myself.

I remember difficult feedback from a close friend about how I was handling my relationships at work. In her own words, "You have to learn that other people do not have your pace, and that is okay. People are different, and the fact that people are not as fast as you are, does not make them dumb." With her feedback, I realised I was stereotyping people, even though I did not have the intention. It was a tipping point for me.

The process of self-knowledge is sometimes challenging and painful, but it is also indispensable. However, you do not have to be alone on this journey. Learn to ask for help when needed. It is also essential to understand that this is a process that we will all go through, eventually, in our lives.

As I like to say, keep learning, keep sharing, and keep growing. Dare to be courageous and challenge your truths constantly. Change your view. Change the direction along the way or adapt to alternative ways. Continue developing and keep going in the face of hardship.

CHARMINE, S. (2012), *Positive Intelligence*, Greenleaf Book Group Press (2012)

GOLEMAN, D., BOYATZIZ, R., MACKEE, A. (2015). "Primal Leadership: The hidden driver of great performance." HBR's 10 Must Reads on Emotional Intelligence. Pages 23-42. Boston, Massachusetts. *Harvard Business Review*.

"Don't Say Anything, Just Listen"

Adesola Orimalade

I arrived in the United Kingdom in early 2006 as an economic migrant, full of expectations, anticipation, and excitement. No, let me explain what I have just said further and put it into perspective.

As a young child, I had a dream to live and work abroad, although Lagos, Nigeria, where my parents raised us, was such a long way from London, New York, Hong Kong, and Singapore. Time never extinguished my desire.

Even at that early age, many of my aspirations were built on my father's foundation. In the late seventies, my father, a civil engineer working for the Nigerian government, was involved in building and maintaining roads and infrastructures across Nigeria. Given the nature of his responsibilities, he came into contact with many expatriates, especially from places like the USSR and Poland. Those interactions translated to him instilling in me the belief and confidence that I could be anything I wanted to be. That colour wasn't a barrier to me living and working successfully anywhere in the world.

I spent many days simply daydreaming about living and working in many of the world's major cities. By the time I finished university, the only way to move abroad for work purposes was to have secured employment, and that was quite challenging.

So, when the UK government introduced the Highly Skilled Migrant Programme, I took advantage and started the journey of making my dream a reality. I had worked for multinationals like Standard Chartered Bank and Citibank in Nigeria; hence I felt I had the right mix of experience and drive to be successful.

I, however, didn't arrive thinking that the streets of the UK were paved with gold or that I wouldn't require a lot of hard work and perseverance to be successful. I was under no illusions that relocating and being successful in a new country was going to be easy. It would require hard work, effort, and determination, but I believed it was the right thing for my daughter and me.

Settling down in London was difficult because although I had a strong background in banking and it was the industry I thought would be most relevant to my background, life doesn't always turn out as we intended. Recruiters and recruitment agencies told me that while I had the correct quantity and quality of experience to work within banking operations (trade finance, treasury, payment), I lacked the proverbial "UK" experience.

My friend then advised me to try searching for a suitable role up north. In his views, "Unlike the people down south, northerners were more welcoming." That turned out to be accurate, but that is a story for another day. So, I moved to Rochdale in Lancashire, not too far from one of the economic centres of Northern England, the historic city of Manchester.

The first role I found was working in finance for Marks & Spencer. Shortly afterwards, I secured a full-time role within credit control for a business-to-business telecommunication service provider in the outskirts of Manchester. The pay wasn't fantastic, but it was the in-road I needed to kick-start my career in the United Kingdom.

My preferred role was to get into corporate treasury and, failing that, corporate banking. These aspirations were still there, but I was determined to step back in order to step forward. The role in credit control was a step back because it was more of an entry-level position. Notwithstanding that, I was enthusiastic and fully committed to being successful at it.

In 2006 and against better judgement, the UK government changed the rules for extending the Highly Skilled Migrant Visa, and it left me with only two options. Either change to a work permit restricting my employment to my current employers, or leave and return home to Nigeria. It was a challenge I wasn't expecting to face. However, there was a third option that I didn't see then, but life has a way of finding new avenues.

Although I was already in full-time employment, I kept receiving viable job opportunities from recruitment agencies, and I had stopped responding. I needed a clear head to decide on which of my two options I was willing to accept. I wasn't worried about returning to Nigeria, although I would have preferred to continue to grow my career in the United Kingdom.

There is a free newspaper published daily in the UK, and I would usually grab a copy at the train station or on the bus each day. The Thursday edition usually had job advertisements, and on that fateful Thursday evening on my way back from work, I grabbed a copy and took it home.

It sat there on my dining table the whole of Friday and, in the evening of that day, I opened it and saw a role in trade finance with a bank based in Manchester. I didn't even know then that the particular bank in question had its office in Manchester. The role itself was perfect for me and mirrored what I had done in the past.

On Sunday evening, I cooked as usual and sat there, watching some programmes on the television. Something urged me to look at the newspaper because the following day, I would have to add it to the usual Monday morning recyclable trash collection. Another part of me thought, "What is the point anyway? Even though you have found a seemingly suitable role, you can't apply because of your visa situation."

Regardless of these conflicting thoughts at dinner that night, I decided to apply, and I did just that. They had placed the job on their website, and I took the time to complete all the required fields and provided a covering letter that I felt evidenced that I met the criteria for the role.

The next day, I went to work as usual. On my return, I checked my laptop. In my inbox was a rejection correspondence from the bank's HR department thanking me for my application and assuring me they had carefully reviewed it. Unfortunately, I didn't meet the criteria of the role. They then wished me the best in my job search.

What other sign did I need to assure me that rather than expending energy searching for a new role, I should focus on deciding whether to apply for a change in my visa status into a work permit restricted to my then-employers or return to Nigeria? The next day went quietly.

Wednesday was like any other day. I went to work and noticed that I had missed a phone call at some point that morning. It was a London number and one I didn't recognise. My initial thought was that one of the many recruitment agencies had contacted me about another job opportunity.

During my lunch break, I stepped out of the principal office building and called the number on my phone. It went to voicemail. The owner of the number had introduced herself as a recruiter calling from the bank I had applied to the previous Sunday. So, I left a message that they could reach me after I left work in the evening.

Later that evening, she called me back and introduced herself. She then told me she noticed I had applied for a role in her organisation. My usual reaction would have been to respond and tell her I had received a rejection email. At that precise moment, a voice spoke to my heart, asking me to be quiet and not say anything. So, I listened and didn't respond. She then told me she would like to invite me for an interview at the Manchester office.

In late 2007, I joined ABN AMRO Bank at their Manchester office, working within trade finance. The journey between that call and my resumption day is another story that I would share one of these days, but now let's pause here and reflect on what I learned.

The first lesson for me is that in life, never stop believing in yourself. If you want other people to believe in you, you must believe in yourself first.

The second lesson, which is perhaps the most important, is I learned the value of listening over speaking. As the years have rolled by, I have always wondered what would have happened if I had interrupted the recruitment officer who called me and told her I had received a rejection email to my application. Some would argue it wouldn't have made a difference, but somehow, I think it would have, if not for any other reasons, perhaps made her pause our conversation to check again.

In life, we are often encouraged to be sharp and quick-witted, and in many of our conversations, we can recollect when we have interrupted others because we "knew where they were going".

As the years have gone by, I realise that we need to slow down and **LISTEN**.

About the Authors

Fatima Alimohamed

Fatima Alimohamed is the CEO of African Brand Warrior and an advocator for Africa and African brands with a solid track record across African markets that lead her to change from boots to heels where needed. Fatima is a thought leader in strategy, brand development, consumer relationships, NPD, marketing and communication.

Fatima's passion is to create brands that make an impact on the end consumers and are tied to the social development of a nation. Her belief is that every contact she makes through her various African markets visit must educate, inspire and help transform the lives of people.

She sat as a Governor on the Kenya Private Sector Alliance (KEPSA), and has been the Chair of the Marketing Society of Kenya, Founder of the Marketing Society East Africa, the Vice President of the Chartered Institute of Marketing Kenya, Chair of the Advertising Standards Committee, Vice President of the Junior Chamber International (JCI) plus a Member of various boards.

Fatima was pulled in by the Founders of Brand Kenya reporting to the President on how to market the country. She has had an illustrious career working with local and international MNCs brands.

Fatima was honoured with the TOP 50 CMOs Global award, TOP 100 Most Talented Marketers, and Iconic Woman Building a Better World by the WEF, among many other international awards. She is stooled as the Queen Mother (Nkosohemaa) in Memia, Western Ghana for her role in social development.

She sits on many boards in Africa and internationally and is an astute speaker at international conferences, schools and universities. Fatima is referenced in various books by international university professors when writing on marketing in Africa.

She supports the Strands of Pearls project on mentoring young African girls on a project titled 'Path of Hope' and is known to be involved in many charity projects.

Get in touch with Fatima:

strateam@gmail.com

www.linkedin.com/in/fatimaalimohamed

Kevin Tong

Growing up between three continents (Taiwan, Cameroon and Switzerland), Kevin is a Swiss, Taiwanese and Hong Kong national and speaks fluent Mandarin, English and French.

Kevin started his early career in various world luxury hotels, then worked as an assistant lecturer in finance and economics for University of Applied Sciences and Arts (HES-SO) in Switzerland. He then joined Pictet & Cie private bank as one of the first three graduates ever selected globally for the wealth management all-around training programme and worked several years in their Geneva headquarters before being transferred internally to Hong Kong in 2007.

He was a Relationship and Portfolio Manager and co-managed a team that managed around one billion USD of UHNWI clients' assets. In 2013, he took an entrepreneurial path and joined IAM Legacy, Family Office as one of the Managing Partners to build a completely new asset management business and lead as team Head of the Business.

Kevin holds a BSc in hospitality management from École Hôtelière de Lausanne (EHL) in Switzerland and an MBA from The University of Chicago Booth School of Business. He is also a CFA Charterholder.

On the personal side, Kevin enjoys exploring the world and has travelled to over sixty-five countries and six continents. He also enjoys participating in various sports at a high level including tennis, basketball, skiing, snowboarding, surfing and diving. He is a NZSIA licenced ski instructor and CASI licensed snowboard instructor, and also holds PADI advanced open water diver and AIDA free diver certificates.

Get in touch with Kevin:

kevintong7@hotmail.com

www.linkedin.com/in/kevin-tong-cfa-7528583

www.instagram.com/kev_t21

Aysha Iqbal

Aysha Iqbal is the Director of Wizz Media, a media and communications training company. She has spent most of her career as a broadcaster and journalist in the UK media.

Aysha began her career working for the national Asian paper, *Asian Xpress*, where she broke a number of exclusive stories, one of which resulted in the reduction in prison sentences for those unjustly sentenced for their role in the Burnley riots. She also received a Sony Gold Award for her work on the Radio 1 documentary 'Vote Friction'.

Following this, Aysha moved in to local radio and later was offered a job at ITV South West as a news presenter and reporter. She was soon headhunted by BBC Spotlight where she was one of the channel's main news presenters and journalists.

As part of her company Wizz Media, Aysha now delivers a variety of workshops from PR training for businesses, to media careers workshops where she shows young media enthusiasts how to reach their goals as a broadcaster/reporter/TV presenter. She also delivers a range of communications workshops in areas such as public speaking, media presentation, and effective communication skills. Aysha currently delivers her training to businesses, councils, educational institutions and youth groups.

Get in touch with Aysha:

info@wizzmedia.co.uk

Lara Rogers

Lara Rogers is a strategic, results-focused executive, with over twenty years' leadership experience gained working with unicorn start-ups, global leaders, and the Life Science sector, specialising in improving operational delivery, customer experience and leading organisational transformation.

Her two greatest passions are placing the customer at the heart of the organisation by being crystal clear about the organisational value proposition, creating innovative and effective customer experience solutions, and supporting the personal development of her teams, empowering them to excel; in particular, mentoring female colleagues to achieve their full potential.

Committed to lifelong learning, Lara has a first class law degree, Legal Practice Course (PGdip), has been a financially regulated person by the FCA, is a GDPR Practitioner, and qualified as a yoga and meditation teacher. Personal memberships have included the Securities Institute, The Solicitors' Regulation Authority, Project Management Professional, and Chartered Institute of Marketers.

A huge advocate of lifelong learning and self-actualisation, Lara is currently studying a postgraduate CIM qualification in Digital Marketing, in addition to undertaking the Lifebook Programme through Mind Valley.

In terms of a current position, Lara has structured her career to enable her to focus on her business passions – customer and patient centricity is the golden thread throughout her career, as is promoting the sustainability of healthcare. She currently works within the Life Science sector for a niche consulting firm, PEN Partnership.

Get in touch with Lara:

larareesrogers3@hotmail.com

Idowu Adebayo Thompson

Idowu Adebayo Thompson is a private wealth expert with over twenty years' banking, wealth management, and financial services experience with very reputable local and offshore institutions such as BMO Bank of Montreal, Standard Chartered Bank and Ecobank Nigeria.

He has worked in several leadership roles covering private wealth, investment advisory and strategy, treasury and financial institutions, capital markets and consumer banking. Idowu has extensive knowledge of wealth management and the high and ultra-high-net-worth client segment business.

His current role is Group Head Private Banking at FirstBank, with the responsibility for the full strategic conception and execution of the private wealth clients' value proposition for the bank's high-net-worth and ultra-high-net-worth clients. Prior to this, he served as Africa Head Investment Advisory and Strategy at Standard Chartered Bank where he was also a member of the Africa Wealth Management Top Team (WMTT) with a direct and matrix oversight for an Investment Advisory team in six countries.

Idowu is a graduate of the University of Lagos and Cardiff Business School MBA programme. He has attended several executive level courses including the Financial Institutions for Private Enterprise Development (FIPED) at the Harvard Business School, Boston and the Finance Programme for Senior Executives at the Said Business School, University of Oxford.

He is also a designated Canadian Seniors Advisor and holds several certifications from the Canadian Securities Institute including the Canadian Securities Course (Honours) and the Professional Financial Planners Course, as well as membership (MCSI) of the Chartered Institute for Securities and Investment in the UK.

Get in touch with Idowu:

www.linkedin.com/in/idowu-thompson-a1113b41

www.facebook.com/idowu.thompson.39

Adaeze Oreh

Dr Adaeze Oreh is a Consultant Family Physician, Senior Health Policy Advisor with the Federal Ministry of Health, and Country Head of Planning, Research and Statistics with Nigeria's National Blood Service Commission.

Between 2009 and 2014, she coordinated a Federal Ministry of Health, United States' Centres for Disease Control and Prevention (CDC), and U.S. President's Emergency Plan for AIDS Relief (PEPFAR) project for blood services in Northern Nigeria. In 2019, Oreh was named one of twenty-five global health and development changemakers awarded the Aspen Institute's New Voices Fellowship.

She is a recipient of the Amujae Leader Award of the Ellen Johnson Sirleaf Presidential Center for Women and Development, and has been named one of Nigeria's 100 Leading Women, one of Nigeria's 100 Most Inspiring Women and listed amongst the Top 100 Career Women in Nigeria.

Adaeze lives in Abuja with her husband, Onwuka Oreh, their two children and five dogs.

Get in touch with Adaeze:

www.twitter.com/Adaeze_Oreh

Junjuan He

Born in China, Junjuan has extensive experience working in Japan as a finance leader in financial management, business leadership, and corporate strategy. She has an excellent ability to work in an extremely complex global environment, and a very structured mind to fit this complexity into transparent and clear frameworks.

As the Senior Finance Director in the world's largest automobile part company, Junjuan plays a key role in controlling the performance of the overseas subsidiaries and joint ventures, including monitoring the set of KPIs for sound management of the performance and the supervision of all cycles of budgeting and forecasting, including modelling and validating business plans.

Prior to this role, Junjuan served as Finance Director for McDonald's Japan where she led successful finance transformations bringing huge improvements in terms of efficiency and cost-savings, and provided insightful finance strategies in the treasury area.

Earlier in her career, Junjuan held senior-level positions in automobile industries for more than ten years, including Honda Motors where she won the presidential awards out of 100,000 candidates for her great working performance.

She is the USCPA license holder, as well as holding a Master of Business Administration from the University of Chicago, Booth School of Business. With a Chinese background and working/education experiences in both Japan and US, she is strong at working in multinational environment and sensitivity to cultural differences.

Get in touch with Junjuan:

www.linkedin.com/in/junjuan-he-8917b6108

Nina Bressler

I was conceived in St Petersburg, born in Vienna in 1980, raised in Boston, and have lived in Prague since 2004. I am a US and Czech citizen.

As a student of transformation throughout my personal and professional life, from my childhood through adulthood, I've had the opportunity to observe people, mindsets and systems as both constraints and enablers of growth and sustainable progress.

Now I'm taking all those learnings and building on them with a purpose in mind in my role as Global Head of Societal Learning at Novartis: To discover new ways to improve and extend people's lives, where learning is a form of medicine.

At the heart of my work is a purpose to help people thrive. I believe that continuous learning, and ethical leadership that is founded on individual autonomy and curiosity unleashes the potential in people, their communities, and their organisations. We are all works in progress, and it is my daily practice to live and work with purpose, be open, be self-aware, serve others, listen to learn, be honest, and continuously seek out opportunities to experiment, thrive, and evolve.

Please connect with me at www.ninabressler.com to follow my personal projects.

Get in touch with Nina:

www.ninabressler.com

www.twitter.com/NinaBressler

www.linkedin.com/in/ninabres

Amelia Samai-Nicome

Amelia Samai-Nicome is responsible for driving value and strategic operations for the T&T IFC. Her experience and leadership have been focused on developing and delivering performance-driven business services and solutions by partnering with company functions to inform better decision-making with robust analysis and critical insight.

She possesses over fourteen years of senior leadership and experience in strategically aligning corporate operations. She has executed the responsibilities of Chief Corporate Officer, Chief Governance Officer and Chief Operations Officer during her tenure.

Amelia has a wealth of experience in cross-functional areas which include operations management, financial management, stakeholder engagement, procurement, human resource management, change management, industrial relations, corporate communications, business development and marketing, HSSE, facilities management, governance, risk, legal, compliance and general administration.

She holds a Bachelor of Science in Economics with a Minor in Human Resource Management from the University of the West Indies. She also holds a triple-accredited MBA from the University of Bradford School of Management. Amelia is also the first Trinidad and Tobago national and the second individual in the Caribbean region to complete the Total Leader Certification from Leadership Management International Inc.

Amelia holds membership in several professional organisations, namely the Leadership Management International (LMI); the Human Resource Management Association of Trinidad & Tobago (HRMATT); the Society of Human Resource Management (SHRM); the Project Management Institute (PMI); and the International Society of Female Professionals (ISFP).

In addition to her cross-section of experience, she is particularly passionate about assisting others in their self-development, career and personal growth journeys, and aims to enrich the lives of anyone with whom she interacts. She lives in Trinidad and Tobago with her husband, two boys and their dogs.

Get in touch with Amelia:

www.amezengroup.com

www.linkedin.com/in/amelia-s-nicome

Shervonne Johnson

Shervonne Johnson's top job is that of CEO of her two lovely children Jaiden (16) and Kyra (14). She is currently the CEO of Mangrove Advisors Ltd, an advisory and consulting firm.

Her career started in the USA as an auditor with Ernst Young, LLP then with American Express Tax & Business Services and RSM McGladrey Consulting Firm. In 2007, after eight exciting and heavy travel-filled years in the US, Shervonne returned home to the Bahamas to work with CitiTrust Bahamas Ltd. as Country Business & Technical Information Security Officer. She served as a Regulator at the Central Bank of the Bahamas and held the post of Regional Risk Manager at Lombard Odier & Cie (Bahamas) Ltd.

Most recently, Ms Johnson served as Director of Risk and Compliance at the Bahamas Power and Light Company (BPL), the largest public utility in the Bahamas. She is considered extremely well rounded in the areas of accounting, enterprise risk management, cross border and data privacy, IT and information security, regulatory compliance, investor liaison and bespoke services.

Shervonne is a graduate of Aquinas College High School and Bethune Cookman University with a Bachelor's degree in Accounting. She is a Certified Information Systems Auditor (CISA) and has a Certification in Information Security Management (CISM). She is a Member of ISACA and the Institute of Internal Audit. She serves as Independent Director on the Board of ST Global Markets and the PACE Foundation. In her college years, she was a former Miss College of the Bahamas (now UB), President of UB Inaugural Rotaract Club and past Vice-President of UB Toastmasters Club.

Shervonne is a Proud Rotarian of the Rotary Club of East Nassau and currently serves as 3rd VP with responsibility for Club Administration. During the pandemic, she organised a community-based initiative Killarney Kares that helped to deliver groceries, pay utilities, find work, provide spiritual and emotional support and more to persons displaced both by Hurricane Dorian and the pandemic. In 2018, Shervonne was honoured to be selected as a Bahamas Financial Services Board (BFSB) Mentor of the Year Nominee.

A key mantra of Shervonne's life is "Leave every place and everyone better than you met them".

Get in touch with Shervonne:

www.linkedin.com/in/shervonne-johnson-cism-cisa-972338

Susana Ecclestone

Susana is Executive Director of the British Argentine Chamber of Commerce (BACC), an organisation that has been promoting bilateral trade and relations between the UK and Argentina since 1995.

She is also part of the Executive Board at FuturED, an educational platform that works towards promoting and creating valuable content for English and Spanish speakers.

She is Director of Hallgarten & Company, an independent mining and energy research firm founded in 2001.

Susana has been part of the working groups on corruption and inclusion and international trade at the B20 Arabia in 2020 and is part of the Executive Board at the Coalition of Green Chambers of Commerce.

Susana is the founder of ShopHuntingDivas, a free platform that promotes emerging fashion designers from all over the world.

In addition, Susana has many years of experience in the private healthcare sector, both in the UK and the

USA. Her varied roles include operations, management, advocacy, political action and international development of skilled and unskilled care services to look after vulnerable children and adults in the comfort of their own homes.

Get in touch with Susana:

www.linkedin.com/in/shophuntingdivas

www.instagram.com/shophuntingdivas

Natasha Preville

Natasha Preville (Bsc, Msc, Dip.) has over twenty-five years' cross-sector experience, with over a decade in senior management within the screen industries, having worked on numerous award-winning campaigns for the BBC and Red Bee Media. Natasha is an advocate and mentor for young people, and is passionate about eradicating barriers to entry for storytellers and young audiences.

She was the Industry Panel Expert for Gen Z Engagement at Google FilmFest 2019. Natasha is part of the TIME'S UP UK movement, working across all sectors to amplify equitable access to opportunity and greater diverse representation in front of and behind the camera.

During her accomplished career, Natasha has remained a keen champion for the transcending role education, sport and culture play in transforming lives. To this end, Natasha founded a consultancy, dedicated to increasing the experience, visibility and tangible career pathways for young people to thrive within the culture, media and sport industries.

Natasha currently acts as Chair for the Association of Panel Members; Independent Director for the National Governing Body for Parkour UK and is a proud Parent Governor.

Get in touch with Natasha:

www.linkedin.com/in/natashapreville

Minal Srivastava

Minal Srivastava has approximately two decades of corporate work experience across multiple product categories and geographies.

She is currently based in India, working in the building material industry.

Minal has won multiple awards, notable among them being Women of Excellence 2019, Women Economic Forum, 50 Most Influential Strategy Leaders 2019, and 50 Most Influential Women 2020.

Beyond work, she is perpetually addicted to Netflix. The only people who can cure her of her addiction are her husband and her nine-year-old son, whom she has produced.

Not that she has produced very many things or beings, but she claims that her son is her greatest production ever!

Whatever time she manages off Netflix and all the work mentioned above, she invests that in trying to help turn her son into a good human being. And write. She dabbles in sharing her joys, failures, frustrations, learnings and vents on the most demanding, difficult, frustrating yet equally fulfilling jobs in the whole world: leadership and parenting.

She succeeds at both – sometimes. Sometimes life takes over.

Get in touch with Minal:

minal.srivastava@gmail.com

www.linkedin.com/in/minal-srivastava-8783082

Natalie Heilling

Natalie Heilling is the Co-Founder and Managing Director of Research Partners, an international research business helping clients find the best talent globally.

She has a BA (Hons) in Design and Media Management and more than twenty years' experience of recruiting and insights. Working with global businesses, Natalie helps to solve recruiting challenges with a particular passion for helping organisations achieve workplace diversity.

Natalie is a Certified Quantum Flow Practitioner. She is passionate about spiritual healing and shares various concepts to help others.

She also has a keen interest in neuroscience, mindset work and personal development. She believes that we can all break free from things that may hold us back, to embody our full potential in every way possible.

Natalie grew up in Hertfordshire, one of three children of bi-racial parents, and spends her time between London and Barbados. She appreciates good food and wine. She loves the ocean and being around highly creative people.

Get in touch with Natalie:

www.linkedin.com/in/natalieheilling

www.instagram.com/natalie.heilling

www.tiktok.com/@natalieheilling

Geri Maroney

Geri Maroney has more than thirty years of business experience in areas including business planning, corporate development, strategic and capital markets, treasury, and tax. She is an innovative problem-solver who is able to combine technical expertise with excellent team building and communication skills to optimise results. She is a respected leader, collaborator, and negotiator.

After a successful career as a treasury executive, Geri is now the Founding Partner of LeanUp, LLC, a mastermind community for treasury professionals. Her company is a private invitation-only community for treasury professionals that is guaranteed to make life easier, as they bring together respected leaders and innovative thinkers to help solve common challenges.

During her executive career, Geri actively participated in large M&A deals, including strategic pre-merger review and due-diligence, multi-billion dollar capital markets and foreign exchange transactions, and global treasury integrations, requiring a high level of technical skill and management expertise to work collaboratively with stakeholders to ensure a smooth and successful project.

In addition, Geri is the published author of *Beautiful Lady*, which is an inspirational guide for women struggling with breast cancer, and is based on her own personal cancer journey. She is a strong advocate for breast cancer awareness and support, and has embarked on a journey to share her story with other cancer warriors to help inspire and encourage them as they fight one of the biggest battles of their life.

Geri has an MBA in International Business and a BS in Business Administration, both from Regis University in Denver, Colorado. She lives in Colorado with her husband, and enjoys travel, golf, hiking, and biking.

Get in touch with Geri:

geri@bebigandbrave.com

Christopher Weguelin

A student of experiential learning, Christopher will honestly admit he spent too much of his education on the sports fields and as a result, started full-time employment at seventeen on a farm.

Over the course of the next fifteen years, he attended college where he gained a diploma in Farm and Business Management before enlisting on a programming course and gaining employment with accounting and ERP software providers.

During the next thirteen years, his career developed from working in a customer support team through project management, team leader, Customer Service Manager and Operations Director.

In 2002, Christopher took the year's break he had never afforded himself and travelled through parts of Asia and Australasia. On his return whilst working for himself, he assisted with a project in Switzerland which in turn led to full-time employment as Process and Quality Manager.

After a brief period as Manager of Accounting, Treasury and Tax, he was promoted to Finance Director for Switzerland with responsibilities for three other central European markets.

His love for the outdoor life has always been an important part of the foundation from which he has built his career, whether it be team sports, or latterly running and cycling including charitable events. Pursuing a level of fitness has been an integral part of his development.

Get in touch with Christopher:

www.linkedin.com/in/cweguelin2019

Gabrielle Botelho

Gabrielle is Global Head of Inclusion & Diversity and HR Director for South America at CGG, where she is leading several HR initiatives aimed at developing a high-performance, people-centered organisational culture, emphasising continuous learning and innovation.

Prior to CGG, Gabrielle worked at Equinor (formerly Statoil) for seven years in different HR managerial positions. In her last role, she oversaw Organization & Leadership Development, working to build the capabilities for the future, digital transformation, and DE&I.

Before Equinor, she was a Senior HR Manager at L'Oréal Brazil.

In the last four years, she has been involved in local and global projects on Diversity, Equity and Inclusion. During 2020, she was the first ever Brazilian speaker at the HR Congress. Her lecture 'DE&I as a Key Pillar of Employer Brand' then became an article published by HRD Connect website.

Gabrielle studied Psychology at Rio de Janeiro Federal University and holds an MBA in Business from FGV-

Rio. She is currently pursuing a Strategic Human Resources Masters' degree from London School. Her line of studying is the model of people-centric organisations and DE&I discipline. She has articles published in Brazil, Portugal, the UK, the USA and Sri Lanka.

Gabrielle is a member of SHRM (Society for Human Resource Management) and a columnist at HR Exchange Network site, where she writes about emotional intelligence.

Get in touch with Gabrielle:

www.linkedin.com/in/gabriellebotelho

Adesola Orimalade

Adesola Orimalade holds a Postgraduate Diploma in Commercial Law from the University of Derby and a BSc degree in Estate Management from the University of Nigeria. He is also a member of the Association of Corporate Treasurers, the Chartered Institute of Management Accountants, and the Chartered Institution of Credit Management.

He has built a successful career first within banking and later moved into Corporate Treasury working with large and medium-sized organisations in Africa and across the European continent.

A published author and avid writer, Adesola enjoys writing for children and young adults. His play, *The First Lady's Poultry*, was published in 2018, and in 2020, he followed that with a colouring book aimed at very young children, *Fruits and Vegetables of the World Coloring Book*. He recently published a picture book *Grandpa's Shoes* for the reading pleasure of children between the age of five and seven years.

In his free time, Adesola enjoys volunteering and currently chairs the Board of Trustees for a charity in the United Kingdom.

Get in touch with Adesola:

www.linkedin.com/in/adesola-harold-orimalade